Tariff Profiles in Latin America

Harry H. Bell

The Praeger Special Studies program—utilizing the most modern and efficient book production techniques and a selective worldwide distribution network—makes available to the academic, government, and business communities significant, timely research in U.S. and international economic, social, and political development.

Tariff Profiles in Latin America

Implications for Pricing Structures and Economic Integration

PRAEGER SPECIAL STUDIES IN INTERNATIONAL ECONOMICS AND DEVELOPMENT

Praeger Publishers New York Washington London

93868

PRAEGER PUBLISHERS
111 Fourth Avenue, New York, N.Y. 10003, U.S.A.
5, Cromwell Place, London S.W.7, England

Published in the United States of America in 1971
by Praeger Publishers, Inc.

© 1971 by Praeger Publishers, Inc.

Library of Congress Catalog Card Number: 75-151948

Printed in the United States of America

In this survey, the author's purpose has been to illustrate some of the insights that analysis of national structures ("profiles") of protection can contribute to the interpretation of current commercial-policy issues in Latin America, particularly with respect to the movement away from national import-substitution policies and toward more-open economies in the context of regional economic integration.

The study views tariffs and other protective measures, not so much as barriers to potential trade flows, but rather in their relative-prices dimension--that is, in terms of their implications for the ratios between domestic and world-market prices.

Drawing on the rapidly growing theoretical literature on nominal and effective protection, the first three chapters stress concepts and methodology of measuring tariffs and quasi-tariffs in order to establish a framework for quantitative evaluations. Thus, it is pointed out that levels of nominal protection (the basic concept for expressing disparities in product prices resulting from or permitted by trade restrictions) are usually measured in terms of the ad valorem percentage height of the customs duties, quota premia, etc., but that it may be more useful to express them in terms of price ratios or implicit exchange rates, especially in Latin America.

Effective protection measures another kind of international price disparity, defined with respect to the value added in a productive process instead of in terms of the price of the end product. By taking account of tariffs on inputs as well as on outputs, this approach emphasizes the fact that the economic effect of protection of intermediate goods is different from that of protection of final goods. The concept is especially useful for assessing incentive and welfare implications of a protective structure.

However, there are formidable statistical problems in measuring nominal and--especially--effective protection. In averaging tariffs, different methods of classification, weighting, sampling, and adjustment of the data may give very divergent numerical results. Where there is "water" in the tariff or where quantitative controls are more important constraints on imports than are customs duties, nominal protection has to be measured by direct comparisons of international and domestic prices that are very difficult to obtain. Indeed, average levels of protection are really interspatial price-index numbers, comparable in many respects to those used in the study of international competitiveness or in calculating the dollar value of other countries' gross national products.

Charts are used not only to clarify the concepts developed but also to illustrate the characteristic features of Latin American protective profiles. One series of charts uses tariff data on Argentina as an example. Another compares the nominal tariff profiles of a number of Latin American countries, as of about 1962, showing not only the prevailing high average rates but also the extreme variability of levels among and within the categories.

Cross-country and intertemporal comparisons of tariff structure are developed further in Chapter 4 by means of experimental use of statistical indicators of average height and relative variability of the tariffs of a number of countries belonging to the Latin American Free Trade Association (LAFTA). These data, based on sampling, give a crude but credible measure of changes in protectionist policies between 1960-62 and 1968.

A common criticism of Latin American protectionist policies is that they lead to inefficient allocation of resources. A review of the concept of comparative advantage (Chapter 5) points out that, under certain assumptions, the ranking of industrial sectors by levels of effective protection is a guide to comparative advantage.

This relationship can be utilized in evaluation of industrial projects, along with programming and other analytical techniques involving estimation of "shadow" prices of products, factors, and foreign exchange. Economists have estimated by static analysis the order of magnitude of the welfare loss incurred by countries that, like many in Latin America, have systematically frustrated their comparative advantage by misplaced or excessive protection. But comparative advantage refers only to specialization as among industrial branches, while account should also be taken of intraindustry specialization, which obeys different rules. This occurs spontaneously under trade liberalization among industrial countries; the LAFTA countries are trying to promote it by ad hoc complementarity agreements. In general, Latin American planners have been interested mainly in manipulating trade policy with a view to so-called dynamic or developmental objectives, but considerations of comparative advantage are now beginning to receive increased attention.

Chapter 6 examines the implications of various characteristics of tariff structure that have been associated with import substitution policies in Latin America; these characteristics include discouragement of exporting, discrimination against agriculture and other primary production, sharp escalation of nominal and effective protection by stages of processing, levying of relatively low duties on sophisticated capital goods, and differentiation of protection on closely related goods that has resulted from application of the indigenous-production criterion or from more or less fortuitous circumstances.

If a common market is the ultimate aim of a regional scheme of economic integration, price levels of internationally traded goods must sooner or later be harmonized within the area. Customs-union theory, which analyzes the effects of this process on efficient allocation of resources in terms of trade diversion and trade creation, is briefly reviewed in Chapter 7 and applied to the Latin American integration objective. Because of Latin America's dependent position in world trade (except with respect to a few primary exports not likely to be affected substantially by integration), it is found that the adverse impact on the rest of the world can be disregarded, unless a Latin American trading bloc were to give discriminatory (reverse) preferences to particular industrialized trading partners. Integration in agriculture would undoubtedly result in substantial net gains from trade creation, but there is no real prospect of this being allowed to occur. In industry, the prospective balance of (static) gains or losses can only be assessed on a product-by-product basis, taking account inter alia of detailed information on present protective structures and of the level of the ultimate common tariffs. In any event, the main reason for Latin American interest in integration is to achieve better economies of scale. Whether this involves trade creation or trade diversion is not considered very relevant.

Certain problems of trade diversion do have political impact on the integration process, however. The claims for special treatment of least-developed member countries are justified in large part by the terms-of-trade loss they are likely to sustain from having to alter a previously outward-looking trade policy and to switch their sources of industrial imports. The problem of depressed areas within countries is analogous. Celso Furtado attributed much of the Brazilian Northeast's difficulties to pressure on that region's intranational terms of trade as a result of industrial protectionism to benefit the Center-South.

The final chapter surveys the institutional framework and the prospects of programs for allocation of industry under Latin American integration schemes. It is noted that the system in the Central American Common Market (CACM) gives "integration" industries monopoly privileges with respect to tariff advantages, and the allocation of such industries involves very difficult negotiations. The LAFTA system, based on complementarity agreements, is an institutionalization of intraindustry specialization without reference to comparative advantage. Both approaches to sector-by-sector integration aim at economies of scale rather than at harmonization of prices and costs. Nevertheless, some efforts are being made, mainly by research institutes, to evaluate the existing disparities in the absolute cost levels and cost structures of particular industries located in various LAFTA countries.

International firms generally welcome regional integration and adapt to it more easily than indigenous firms. However, partly because the integration-industry and complementarity regimes involve special privileges, Latin Americans are likely to exert greater pressure for the formation of joint ventures in the context of integration. The problem of locus of control becomes more acute as host countries move away from national-level import substitution and look outward to regional integration or expansion of nontraditional exports to third countries, even though it is precisely in these circumstances that--from the point of view of the international firm--centralized managerial responsibility based on 100 per cent control is thought to be of strategic importance. In any case, there is now much political pressure for creation of Latin American multinational enterprises, in which governments and private firms of several Latin American countries would share control, relegating extrazonal companies to at most a minority role.

More detailed study and better data are needed in order to apply tariff-profile analysis to the myriad problems of moving toward a Latin American common market through systematic (i.e., across-the-board) reduction of barriers to intratrade and alignment on a common external tariff. Confrontation of the tariff structures of different combinations of countries and subgroupings (Andean Group, the CACM, the River Plate countries, and perhaps the Caribbean Free Trade Association) might indicate the relative feasibility of various proposed scenarios of integration. Certain tentative conclusions in this regard are nevertheless broached at the end of Chapter 8.

This study is based on a report of a similar title prepared by the author with support from the U.S. Department of State. The author is solely responsible for its contents, including the accuracy of both statements of fact and interpretive comments.

Grateful acknowledgment is also made of cooperation received from a number of officials of various governments and international organizations, as well as members of research institutions in Latin America and the United States who provided valuable background information and documentation, but who would not necessarily agree with the author's interpretations. Useful comments and criticisms on portions of the draft were received from--among others--Antonin Basch, Isaiah Frank, Peter T. Knight, Constantine Michelopolous,

Raymond Mikesell, Charles Pearson, Scott Pearson, Herbert F. Propps, and Wolfgang Renner; but they of course share no responsibility for factual or analytical errors remaining in the final version.

Special thanks are due to Cameron L. Pippitt for statistical, bibliographic, editorial, and other assistance in preparation of the original version of the paper and to Barbara Mercer for her indispensable collaboration in a previous project that was closely related to this one.

xi

Chapter

Chapter

LIST OF TABLES

LIST OF CHARTS

LIST OF ABBREVIATIONS

AID — Agency for International Development

ALALC — Asociación Latinoamericana de Libre Comercio

BTN — Brussels tariff nomenclature

CACM — Central American Common Market

CAP — Common agricultural policy

CARIFTA — Caribbean Free Trade Association

CEMLA — Centro de Estudios Monetarios Latinoamericanos

CEPAL — Comisión Económica para América Latina

CXT — Common external tariff

ECIEL — Estudios Conjuntos sobre Integración Económica Latinoamericana (Program of Joint Studies on Latin American Economic Integration)

ECLA — Economic Commission for Latin America

EEC — European Economic Community

FIEL — Fundación de Investigaciones Económicas Latino-americanas (Buenos Aires)

GATT — General Agreement on Tariffs and Trade

IBRD — International Bank for Reconstruction and Development

IDES — Instituto de Desarrollo Económico y Social (Buenos Aires)

ILPES	Instituto Latinamericano de Planificación Económica y Social
INTAL	Instituto para la Integración de América Latina (Buenos Aires)
IPEA	Instituto de Pesquisa Econômico-Social Aplicada
ipr	Implicit price ratio
LAFTA	Latin American Free Trade Association
MFN	Most-favored-nation
NBER	National Bureau of Economic Research
OECD	Organization for Economic Cooperation and Development
SITC	Standard International Trade Classification
TVA	Tax on value added
UNIDO	United Nations Organization for Industrial Development
UNCTAD	United Nations Conference on Trade and Development

Tariff Profiles in Latin America

CONCEPTS OF PROTECTION

The study of commercial policy has been transformed almost
beyond recognition during the last decade by the introduction of a new
terminology and by substantial redefinition of familiar concepts. This
reformulation mainly results from recent interest of economists in
so-called effective protection.

Effective protection is discussed further in Chapter 2. For the
moment let it be defined as a measure of the net incidence (positive
or negative) that tariffs and other protective measures have on the
value added to a good by a particular production activity. Protective
measures include customs duties and subsidies on imports and exports,
quantitative trade restrictions, certain internal taxes and the related
compensatory border taxes and rebates, multiple exchange rates, and
any other forms of governmental discrimination between domestic and
foreign production, except direct subsidies to domestic producers.[1]
As will be seen, in calculating effective tariffs, account is taken not
only of the tariff applicable to the output of a given productive process,
but also of the effect on cost of production resulting from the tariffs,
etc., applicable to the material inputs.

The term "nominal protection" has been given to the more con-
ventional approach, which refers to the incidence that tariffs and such
protective measures have with respect to the price of particular
products. Calculations of nominal protection take account only of the
tariffs and other protective measures applicable to a given output
and ignore the effects of the protective system on its input costs.

The new emphasis has affected the way economists look at
"protection" in general. The word itself is, unfortunately, loaded

1

with commercial-warfare connotations. To protectionists it has meant
the erection of defensive barriers against invasion by foreign goods.
Free-traders have also stressed the restrictive aspect of the tariff
and nontariff barriers. When it came to quantitative measurement of
the height of a tariff, it was often assumed that what one wanted to
evaluate was some index of its restrictive effect[2] defined in terms of
its impact (e.g., the difference between a country's actual imports and
its potential imports in the absence of restrictions) or in terms of the
increase in domestic production made possible by the restrictions.
All such estimates require very sophisticated calculations which take
account of foreign and domestic elasticities of supply and demand.

As a by-product of the studies of effective protection, however,
it is now becoming customary to define and measure nominal protection
primarily in terms of the implications for relative price levels and
not primarily in terms of restrictiveness. Thus, in the World Bank's
study of the structure of protection, "the nominal rate of protection
of a particular commodity is defined as the percentage of domestic
over world market prices, resulting from the application of protective
measures."[3] Current studies of effective protection always start
from the assumption that the domestic price of each product, net of
domestic taxes and subsidies, is exactly equal to the world price plus
the tariff that is or would be paid to import it. To be sure, this assumption will not be literally verifiable in practice. At any given time, the
actual observed price of a domestic good may well diverge substantially
from that which would be predicted from the international price of a
corresponding imported good plus customs charges. Allowance must
be made for product differentiation, for consumer tastes favoring the
foreign over the domestic product or vice versa, for temporary market
disequilibria, for noncomparability of markups at the wholesale stage,
etc. In its simplified formulation, the definition also assumes that the
customs duty is not so high as to exclude all foreign competition and
that there are no quantitative restrictions or monopolistic market
structures.

One advantage of defining "protection" in terms of its price
effects is that it makes all types of protective measures (tariffs,
subsidies, quotas, etc.) commensurate. Another advantage is that,
by shifting attention from the barriers themselves to the relative-
price structures that they imply, it avoids the usual overpreoccupation
with the economic-warfare aspects of commercial policy and focuses
more analysis on such internal effects of protection as distortion of
domestic terms of trade between industry and agriculture, discouragement of exports, and concealed subsidization of inefficient producers.
To be sure, the price definition of protection is still not accepted by
all recent writers. F. D. Holzman[4] argues for its definition in terms
of the impact of protective measures on trade flows, measured against

some criterion--such as the gross national product--that reflects the
importing country's capacity to bear the burden of import competition.
In rebuttal, it can be pointed out that such impact estimates always
have to be calculated from information on relative-price effects in
any case. It would appear to be more useful, as well as simpler, to
give priority to measuring protection in its price dimension.

TARIFFS AND IMPLICIT PRICE RATIOS

One can express levels of nominal protection either in terms of
tariff rates (as an ad valorem percentage of cif prices, where imports
are concerned) or directly in terms of the price ratios between domestic and foreign prices, taking the cif import price as unity. As has
been mentioned above, however, actual scheduled tariffs (including
customs duties and other protective measures of equivalent effect--
such as import surcharges--that are directly incorporated in landed
prices) frequently do not correspond to the observed price disparities.
In measuring protection, therefore, although it is usually easier to
work from the tariff schedule, it would be more appropriate to work
from direct price comparisons if these were obtainable (which is
unfortunately seldom the case). In order to avoid confusion, we shall
sometimes use the term ' "implicit price ratio" (ipr) to designate that
ratio between domestic and foreign prices expressed in international
currency at a given rate of exchange that would correspond to an ad
valorem tariff rate (t) as derived, say, from the schedule of customs
duties. The term "implicit tariff" (ℓ) will be used to express the
percentage of price differential that would correspond to a directly
measurable price ratio (pr).

Thus, for the ith good (and ignoring domestic indirect taxes):

$$\text{ipr} \quad = \quad \frac{1 + t_i}{1} \quad = \quad 1 + t_i$$

$$\ell \quad = \quad \frac{P_{i\,(d)} - P_{i\,(f)}}{P_{i\,(f)}}$$

$$\text{pr} \quad = \quad \frac{P_{i\,(d)}}{P_{i\,(f)}} \quad = \quad \frac{1 + \ell_i}{1} = \quad 1 + \ell_i$$

Comparing tariffs (t) with implicit tariffs (ℓ), or price ratios
(pr) with implicit price ratios (ipr), yields important information.
When the implicit price ratios derivable from the schedule of customs
duties, surcharges, etc., are substantially higher than the measurable
price ratios, the tariff is redundant: it contains "water" and is not

fully utilized. This may occur when the scheduled import tariff was
set so high as to be prohibitive; however, it may also result from
successful import-substitution policies where domestic competition
has lowered prices to such an extent that an originally nonredundant
tariff has become prohibitive. Among Latin American countries,
Chile furnishes many examples of the first type of redundancy; Mexico,
of the second type. In both these countries, and in many others, one
must make at least some direct price comparisons in order to draw
meaningful welfare statements about the protective structures. Nevertheless, the implicit price ratios derived from tariff schedules are
themselves important measures of the potential protection that will be
fully utilized after further domestic inflation eliminates redundancy or
in the event of a fall in the international prices of the commodities in
question.

EXPORT TAXES AND SUBSIDIES

Thus far, the discussion of nominal protection has referred only
to the positive protection of imports. Negative nominal protection in
the form of subsidization of imports is possible, but rare. Negative
and positive nominal protection on exportable goods, usually in the
form of taxes on traditional exports and of subsidies on nontraditional
exports, are common but seldom show the pronounced amplitudes of
variation that characterize import tariffs. Most potential nontraditional
exports of Latin American countries appear to have zero or--where
there are subsidies in the form of customs "drawbacks"--relatively
much lower protection than is indicated by the tariff applied to a
similar imported goods. Consideration of a country's structure of
nominal tariffs should cover all tradable goods--exportables as well
as importables. Unfortunately, it is often difficult to obtain information
on a country's export regime in a form consistent with the classification
of its import regime. That is why it is frequently assumed, incorrectly,
that there is zero protection on exports--i.e., that domestic and world
prices are at parity, allowing for freight.

INTERNAL INDIRECT TAXES AND
BORDER COMPENSATION

Once protection is defined in terms of the commodity-by-com-
modity disparities between domestic and international prices at a
given rate of exchange, it is apparent that one should also make
adjustments to allow for effects of the domestic indirect tax system
on relative prices. Following the usual assumption (admittedly not
always valid) that indirect taxes are fully shifted forward into the
price of the product, while direct taxes are borne by the factors of

production, an excise tax on production of exportables and import-substitutables reduces nominal protection correspondingly, while the reimbursement of indirect taxes on exports increases correspondingly the nominal protection on domestically produced goods. If all goods consumed in the country bear indirect taxation at the same ad valorem rate and if border-tax measures (export reimbursements and compensatory taxes on imports) are also applied consistently across the board, the tax system is neutral and the portion of the price disparity between domestic and foreign goods resulting from the indirect taxes can be ignored in evaluating the system of protection.* An approximation to such neutrality might result if a tax on value added (TVA), such as is being adopted in the European Economic Community, were to be applied in rigorous consistency with the rules of the destination principle, according to which the entire incidence of indirect taxes is made to fall in the country consuming the goods. In practice, equality between the incidence of tax domestically levied and the rate of adjustment at the frontier may not be achieved across the board for all tradable goods, even with the TVA. With the "cascade" type of turnover tax, such as was formerly used in the Federal Republic of Germany, it is technically impossible for full neutrality to be achieved. Theoretically, therefore, any differentiated system of indirect tax measures should be fully accounted for, positively and negatively, in evaluating a country's pattern of protection. There are statistical difficulties, however, in getting indirect tax data consistent with the classification used for customs data, even in advanced countries. The result is that indirect taxes are frequently disregarded, except in computing effective protection, in which case ignoring them might seriously distort the results.[5]

QUANTITATIVE RESTRICTIONS

The protective measures discussed above have been those which, like ordinary customs duties on imports, directly drive a wedge between domestic and foreign prices. To these can be added advanced deposits on imports, the interest cost of which can also fairly easily be converted into ad valorem tariff equivalents. But what about such nontariff barriers as import and export prohibitions, import and export licensing, administrative restrictions justified on sanitary

---

*It is not neutral with respect to the exchange rate. (See The High Authority of the European Coal and Steel Community, Report on the Problems Raised by the Different Turnover Tax Systems Applied Within the Common Market ["Tinbergen Report," Luxembourg, 1953], p. 24.)

grounds, state trading, and those restrictive practices that result
from private monopoly of channels of import distribution and export
commercialization? Here the evaluation must depend on direct
comparison of domestic and foreign prices. The presumed contribution
of the quasi-tariffs to total protection is shown by any excess of the
observed price ratios over the implicit price ratios derived from the
tariff and--where domestic indirect taxes and border taxes must be
taken into account--the tax schedule. (It is recalled that any excess
in the other direction indicates redundancy in the protective structure.)
Depending on the availability of comparative price information, it is
also possible to analyze the commercial policy of Communist countries
in terms reasonably comparable to those used for market-economy
countries. However, this comparability may be vitiated to the extent
that--because of repressed inflation--the prices set by the authorities
of such countries do not approximate the market-clearing prices.

At one time or another, most Latin American countries have
used import licensing and other nonprice measures which, when
effective, superseded the tariff-like measures as determinants of
price disparities. Thus, in Mexico, out of 40 industrial sectors
studied for 1960, the nominal tariff rates indicated by observed price
ratios were higher than the apparent nominal tariff rates in 17 sectors
and equal in two sectors. For the 21 other sectors, however, price
comparisons indicated that both the tariff system proper and the
quota controls were redundant.[6]

NOMINAL PROTECTION AND EXCHANGE RATES

The approach to nominal protection described up to now has
been based on observed or implicit international price comparisons
where both the internal price and the world price are expressed in
the same currency (normally foreign currency) and the exchange rate
is assumed to be given. This is all very well when dealing with industrial countries, which only seldom change their parities. However,
for many Latin American countries, in which there is a permanent
race between domestic inflation and exchange depreciation, or where
there are various multiple exchange rates, it is impossible to avoid
looking at the exchange-rate aspect of protection.

The Tariff Equivalent of Multiple Exchange Rates

Multiple exchange rates can be expressed in terms of tariffs
or implicit tariffs just like any other protective measures that operate
directly on relative prices. The difference between the basic rate of
exchange, if there is one, and the special rate applied to a given

category of imports or exports is simply added to or subtracted from
the legal tariff. But a problem will arise in most multiple-rate structures as to which rate is the basic one. In such cases, one can select
as the basic rate whichever of the rates above the official parity seems
to account for most transactions, or even the highest free-market rate,
but any such choice will be just as arbitrary as the official rate (with
the extra disadvantage that all the other tariffs and subsidies will have
to be recomputed from the base chosen).

It is virtually impossible to draw the line between those import
surcharges and special taxes that are part of the customs-duty system
and those that are multiple exchange rates. The distinction is for
many purposes irrelevant, but it can usually be drawn on the basis of
the administrative agency under whose authority the surtax or premium
is levied. Thus, if the central bank buys and sells foreign exchange at
several different prices, it is a multiple-exchange-rate practice, even
though the end result as far as the cost of imports and proceeds of
exports are concerned is identical to that which might have been
obtained from some combination of import and export duties and
subsidies administered by the Finance Ministry and involving budgetary
receipts and disbursements. There may, to be sure, be a substantive
fiscal difference, depending on the central bank's relationship to the
Treasury with respect to disposition of any local-currency profit or
loss from dealings in exchange. Moreover, if certain import and
export transactions are routed through a free, "gray," or "black"
market, e.g., where importers of nonessential goods obtain their
foreign exchange directly from nontraditional exporters, the exchange
premium will bypass the authorities entirely.

At one time or another all the independent countries of South
America have had multiple-rate structures, providing differentiated
treatment for different types of exports and imports. This was moti-
vated in part to promote specific industrialization goals and in part to
tax the export sector; in part it was merely the result of a series of
ad hoc arrangements in which governments were following the line of
least resistance in response to the fluctuating political power of industrial and agricultural interests. Piecemeal adjustment of an overvalued
official exchange rate to domestic inflation, avoiding the onus of outright
devaluation, also played a role. During recent years, the multiple-rate
regimes have been simplified or eliminated in a number of the countries
(Argentina, Bolivia, Brazil, Colombia, Chile, and Venezuela), at least
with respect to visible trade. Exchange recargos (surcharges) are
still applied to imports in Ecuador, Paraguay, Peru, and Uruguay; in
these countries they should be added in along with tariffs as "price"
measures.[7] Uruguay has the most confusing system, under which
various imports are subject to regular customs duties, additional
duties, the additional special duty, the extraordinary "patent,"

surtaxes on the customs duties and special duties, the special tax, exchange surcharges, and several different requirements for advance deposits.

The Uniform Exchange-Rate Equivalent of a Tariff Structure

This leads to the general problem of how to distinguish between that portion of a tariff level which should be considered protection and that portion which should be attributed to the exchange rate. Clearly, there is no essential difference, as far as merchandise trade and the real economy are concerned, between, on the one hand, an import tariff rate of 100 per cent matched by a 100 per cent subsidy on all exports and, on the other hand, a devaluation that doubles the rate of exchange. Moreover, any differentiated protective tariff structure could theoretically be replaced by some undifferentiated exchange rate with no net impact on the balance of payments. In this connection, one of the many possible ways of averaging tariffs is the devaluation equivalent, which is the percentage devaluation that would be required to restore external balance if all existing tariffs (as well as all export subsidies and taxes) were removed.[8]

Adjustment for Currency Overvaluation

Since the official exchange rates of national currencies in Latin America and other developing countries are usually considered overvalued in various degrees, it can be misleading to make international and intertemporal comparisons of the height of protection as measured by the apparent tariff rates. One solution to this problem is to measure positive or negative tariff rates from a zero mark based on the world market price converted, not at the existing exchange rate, but rather at the exchange rate that would prevail under free trade. The empirical estimation of this imaginary bench mark involves solving a general equilibrium system of equations requiring input-output information and estimates of the elasticities and cross-elasticities of supply and demand for the various categories of goods. The next step is to adjust all the observed rates of protection to put them in terms of the hypothetical equilibrium exchange rate thus calculated. Balassa and Associates used this procedure to obtain adjusted net rates of nominal and effective protection for several countries. In each case this resulted in lowering substantially the apparent rates of protection shown.[9]

This is a very elaborate exercise, one policy-makers have to go through when a government actually contemplates setting a new

rate of exchange in conjunction with a thoroughgoing reform of the
entire tariff structure (especially in the case of a compensated devaluation). Estimation of the hypothetical equilibrium exchange rate and
calculation of net rates of nominal or effective tariffs are also necessary
when comparing effects of protection on traded vs. nontraded goods,
and in applying certain techniques of project evaluation. For most
purposes of international comparison of protective structure, however,
calculation of the equilibrium exchange rate is hardly worth the trouble,
in view of the fact that any results obtained are very ephemeral,
especially in Latin America. For such purposes, there is an easier
solution.

Protection is defined in terms of the implications of protective
measures for relative price levels. These can be measured as well
by comparing one price ratio or implicit price ratio with another as
by comparing rates of tariff. As far as the relationship among tradable
commodities is concerned, the interproportionality among the price
ratios or of implicit price ratios, as well as their sector-by-sector
rank ordering, is invariant with respect to changes in the exchange
rate used in setting the zero tariff rate. For most analytical purposes
involving protection (as distinguished from purposes involving the
balance of payments), there is no need to adjust for the degree of over-
or undervaluation of the currency, provided the levels of protection
are expressed in price-ratio terms rather than in terms of tariff
rates. As an illustration of this point, it may be noted that Balassa's
estimates of adjusted net nominal and effective rates yield the same
ratios among the corresponding implicit price ratios as do the unad-
justed rates.[10]

Implicit Exchange Rates

When considering the joint effect of nominal protection, domestic
inflation, and exchange depreciation, it is convenient to take the ratios
between domestic wholesale prices in local currency and foreign
prices in international currency. This gives implicit exchange rates
instead of implicit price ratios. Instead of showing multiple exchange
rates as if they were elements of the tariff structure, tariffs and
quasi-tariffs are shown as if they were elements of a multiple-exchange-
rate structure. This concept of implicit exchange rates has been used
notably by Stephen R. Lewis, Jr.[11] in a series of studies on Pakistan
and by Paul G. Clark in his studies on Brazil.[12]

At any given point in time, the implicit exchange rate for a
product equals the implicit price ratio multiplied by the exchange
rate. The profile of implicit exchange rates is therefore identical to
the profile of implicit price ratios, except for a scale factor. Over

time, however, implicit exchange rates will tend to rise, accompanying
exchange-rate depreciation or devaluations, upward tariff changes,
and inflationary increases in domestic prices of tradable goods to the
extent these are not offset by parallel rises in world prices.

EXAMPLES OF PROFILES OF NOMINAL PROTECTION

The concepts just discussed are illustrated by reference to
Charts 1 through 14.

Common External Tariff, European
Economic Community

Chart 1 summarizes information on the European Economic
Community's common external tariff schedules (CXT) as they stood
before and after the Kennedy Round negotiations. Divisions along the
horizontal axis show, in numerical order, the one digit sections and
principal two-digit chapters of the Standard International Trade
Classification (SITC), Sections 0 through 8. Relative importance of
the commodity classifications is indicated by the horizontal spacing,
which is proportionate to total Organization for Economic Cooperation
and Development (OECD) imports in 1965 (used as a proxy for world
trade). The profile of the diagram shows estimated average levels of
nominal tariffs (including zero duties), without adjustment for domestic
indirect taxation or for the corresponding border-taxes. The estimator
used for each classification was the arithmetic mean of a stratified
randomized sample of individual items, the sample being self-weighted
in approximate proportion to total OECD imports in 1965. The full
sample, which is the one used by the UNCTAD Secretariat in its study
of the results of the Kennedy Round negotiations,[13] comprises 504
items. The sample is not used, however, for most of SITC Section 0
(foodstuffs), in view of the fact that the UNCTAD Kennedy Round study
did not attempt to measure the ad valorem incidence of the variable
levies and other special protective devices applied by the EEC under
its common agricultural policy (CAP). The 52 per cent level of nominal
tariff indicated on Chart 1 for supported agricultural items reflects
an average of the estimated implicit tariffs (i.e., based on direct
comparisons of domestic with international prices) in the four customs
areas of the EEC in 1963-64, before the CAP market regulations were
fully in place and before unified target prices were established.[14]

Average levels of nominal protection can be read from the chart
either in terms of ordinary tariff rates (percentage points), by using
the right-hand scale (on which the zero mark represents the cif international price of imports), or in terms of implicit price ratios, by

CHART 1

Profiles of Nominal Tariffs: EEC Common External Tariff,
Before and After Kennedy Round
(weighting based on "world trade," i.e., total
OECD imports, 1965)

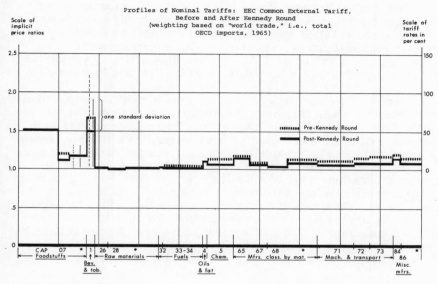

CAP	Common agricultural policy
*	Other
07	Tropical products
1	Beverages and tobacco
4	Oils and fat
5	Chemicals
26	Textile fibers
28	Ore and scrap
32	Coal
33-34	Oil and gas

65	Textiles
67	Iron and steel
68	Nonferrous
71	Nonelectrical machinery
72	Electrical machinery
73	Transport equipment
84	Clothing
86	Instruments, etc.

Source: Except for items subject to common agricultural policy (CAP), averages and standards deviations have been calculated from the 504-item sample used by UNCTAD in TD/6/Rev. 1, The Kennedy Round: Estimated Effects on Tariff Barriers.

using the left-hand scale (on which the cif import price is normalized
as unity). The two measures give different ways of looking at the
overall results of the EEC's tariff reductions in the Kennedy Round.
For example, in tariff terms, EEC concessions are estimated to
reduce average tariffs on manufactures (SITC's 5 through 8) by an
average of about 36 per cent. This is of interest mainly as it compares
with the original Kennedy Round objective of a 50 per cent "linear cut."
In implicit-price-ratio terms, the concessions imply about 4 percent
reduction in the ratios between prices of manufactures within EEC
and international prices. This type of calculation is useful, in conjunction with estimated or assumed price elasticities of substitution,
in making projections of incremental trade attributed to tariff charges.

Among the shortcomings of using a set of tariff averages to
represent the whole frequency distribution of a protective structure
is the loss of information on the degree of item-by-item variation
within the categories averaged. Indeed, variations within a category
are quite likely to be greater in amplitude than are variations among
categories. Since the variation of individual rates is in itself an
important characteristic of a tariff system, further description of the
frequency distribution of the sample is desirable. In this chart, therefore, the sample standard deviations are represented by the lengths
of the thin lines, which extend one standard deviation above and one
below the averages. The EEC external tariff structure is relatively
smooth, compared to that of other industrial countries, largely because
it came into being through the averaging of four separate tariff systems.

Argentina, Before and After the 1967 Reforms

For a striking contrast with the EEC tariff, we turn now to a
typical case of Latin American protectionism: the tariff structure of
Argentina before the tariff and exchange reform of 1967. The averages
and standard deviations portrayed in Chart 2 are based on the same
sample items and the same weighting system used for Chart 1, but
the vertical scale is only half that of Chart 1 because of the much
greater amplitude of variation. The peak average on Chart 2 is an
ad valorem tariff rate (actually, tariffs plus recargos) of 321 per cent
(ipr of 4.2) in SITC 84 (Clothing). If certain additional import taxes*
and the cost of tying up credit for advance import deposits** were

----

*The principal omissions are: statistical tax (1.5 per cent) and
consular tax (1.5 per cent).

**Most imports require a six-months advance deposit of 40

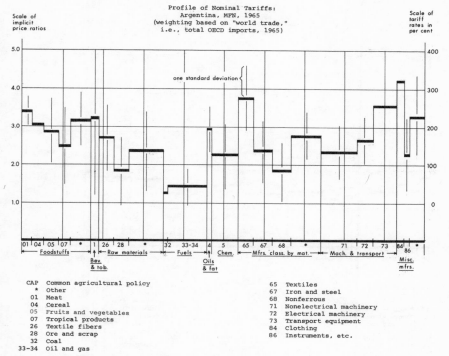

CHART 2

Profile of Nominal Tariffs:
Argentina, MFN, 1965
(weighting based on "world trade,"
i.e., total OECD imports, 1965)

Scale of
implicit
price ratios

Scale of
tariff
rates in
per cent

one standard deviation

| 01 | 04 | 05 | 07 | * | 1 | 26 | 28 | * | 32 | 33-34 | 4 | 5 | 65 | 67 | 68 | * | 71 | 72 | 73 | 84 | * |

Foodstuffs   Bev. & tob.   Raw materials   Fuels   Oils & fat   Chem.   Mfrs. class. by mat.   Mach. & transport   Misc. mfrs. 86

CAP	Common agricultural policy		65	Textiles
*	Other		67	Iron and steel
01	Meat		68	Nonferrous
04	Cereal		71	Nonelectrical machinery
05	Fruits and vegetables		72	Electrical machinery
07	Tropical products		73	Transport equipment
26	Textile fibers		84	Clothing
28	Ore and scrap		86	Instruments, etc.
32	Coal			
33-34	Oil and gas			

Source: Calculated, using 504-item UNCTAD sample, from surcharge (recargo) rates shown in Nomenclatura Arancelaria y Recargos de Importación, 1965.

13

CHART 3

Profile of Nominal Tariffs:
Argentina, MFN, 1967
(weighting based on "world trade,"
i.e., total OECD imports, 1965)

Scale of
implicit
price ratio

Scale of
tariff
rates in
per cent

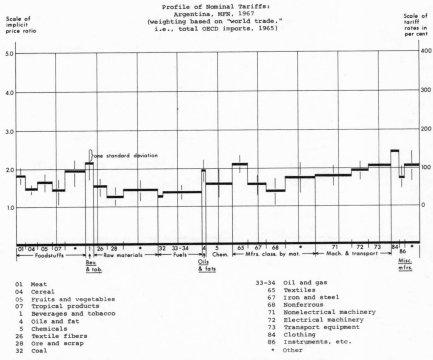

01 Meat
04 Cereal
05 Fruits and vegetables
07 Tropical products
 1 Beverages and tobacco
 4 Oils and fat
 5 Chemicals
26 Textile fibers
28 Ore and scrap
32 Coal

33-34 Oil and gas
  65 Textiles
  67 Iron and steel
  68 Nonferrous
  71 Nonelectrical machinery
  72 Electrical machinery
  73 Transport equipment
  84 Clothing
  86 Instruments, etc.
   * Other

Source: Calculated, using 504-item UNCTAD sample, from surcharge (recargo) rates shown in
Nomenclador Arancelario Aduanero, No. 9 (July-August, 1969).

14

included, the averages would be somewhat higher, but the ranking
would probably not change. The variation of individual rates in the
prereform Argentine tariff is indicated by a standard deviation of 109
percentage points for all sampled manufactured goods (SITC's 5 through
8), corresponding to a coefficient of variation of 0.4 with respect to
average implicit prices ratios. Comparable figures for the EEC
(after the Kennedy Round) were 8 percentage points and a coefficient
of variation of 0.05. The scope of the 1967 reform of the Argentine
nominal tariff structure can be seen by comparing Charts 2 and 3.
The reform more than halved nominal import tariff rates, from the
overall ad valorem average for manufactures of 173 per cent to 81
per cent (still as measured by the standard 504-item sample).* The
average in the peak category came down from 321 per cent to 140
per cent (ipr of 2.4). Perhaps more important, the variation within
categories was greatly reduced. The sample standard deviation for
manufactures (SITC's 5-8), while still much greater than in the industrial countries, is now 40 percentage points of tariff, representing a
coefficient of relative variation of 0.22 with respect to average implicit
price ratios. Furthermore, although the amplitude of variation from
category to category is still much greater than in the industrial
countries, the rank ordering of the various commodity categories
with respect to levels of nominal protection is now quite close to that
in the EEC, which--as far as nonagricultural goods are concerned--
is generally typical of tariff structure in industrial countries. Whereas
the Argentine protective regime that existed before 1967 had been the
product of historical accident, with relatively little apparent inner
logic, the reformed tariff was inspired by policy principles that resulted
in a pattern of escalation similar to that which had evolved in Western
Europe.

The Kennedy Round cuts in the industrial countries' tariffs
averaged considerably less than 50 per cent and are being spread
over five years. How could Argentina's tariffs be cut by a more
drastic percentage, from much higher levels, and so suddenly, without
bankrupting all the country's import-substitution industries? The
answer is, of course, that the reduction in internal (peso) prices
implied by the tariff cuts was offset by the simultaneous devaluation

---

per cent of import value. Since the marginal cost of credit runs from
2 to 3 per cent per month, the additional incidence resulting from this
requirement is about 6 per cent ad valorem.

*If the Argentine tariff reform of 1967 were viewed in the
context of the Kennedy Round--rather than as a self-help measure--
Argentina's "performance" would exceed that of any other country.

of the peso, from 250 to 350 to the U.S. dollar. (The existence of
substantial redundancy in the prereform tariff also had a cushioning
effect.) The relative-price ceilings implied jointly by the tariff reform
and the devaluation are shown in terms of implicit exchange rates
(pesos to the dollar) in Chart 4. The superimposed profiles, before
and after the tariff/exchange reform, show that the smoothing-out of
the pattern of protection did not change very radically the general
level of implicit exchange rates for imports and import-substitutes.

Meanwhile, on the export side, the imposition of a system of
graduated export taxes, with rates up to 25 per cent, absorbed some
of the windfall profit that would have been received by exporters of
meat and other traditional Argentine export products after the basic
exchange rate at which they convert their proceeds rose from 250 to
350 pesos to the dollar. Exporters of nontraditional products benefited
immediately from the exchange-rate realignment.

Since the profiles of protection depicted in these charts are
based on the published import tariff schedule and not on direct observation of the ratios between domestic and foreign prices, it is necessary
to seek other information in order to evaluate the element of actual
redundancy. Table 1 shows for certain nontraditional Argentine export
products (1) the legal nonpreferential ad valorem tariff, (2) the actual
percentage price differential between domestic and international prices
(calculated fob, because we are dealing here with exports), (3) the
percentage of drawback (export subsidy) calculated on the international
price, and (4) whether or not Argentine exports of the product benefit
from preferences in LAFTA-partner countries. In some of the above
cases, notably in the agricultural sector, it can be seen that Argnetina's
ability to export is based on an outright price advantage. In others,
the price disadvantage indicated in Column 2 is offset in whole or
in part by the drawback received by the exporter and/or by a preferential advantage in a LAFTA market. Finally, there are some cases
where a residual price disadvantage presumably has to be offset
against higher profits from sales in the protected domestic market.

Argentina, Margins of Intra-LAFTA Preference

The profiles of the protection implied by the Argentine tariff
schedules illustrated thus far refer only to most-favored-nation
tariffs. However, lower rates of duty are being applied to trade with
LAFTA partners. In evaluating progress made toward Argentina's
trade liberalization toward the rest of Latin America, it is of interest
to look at the magnitude and patterns of the margins of intra-LAFTA
preferences (Chart 5).

CHART 4

Profiles of Implicit Exchange Rates:
Argentina, 1965 and 1967
(weighting based on "world trade,"
i.e., total OECD imports, 1965)

Scale of
implicit
exchange rates
mn/US1.00

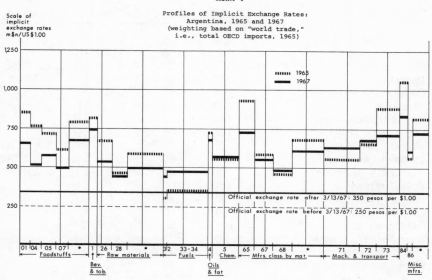

········ 1965
▬▬▬ 1967

Official exchange rate after 3/13/67: 350 pesos per $1.00

Official exchange rate before 3/13/67: 250 pesos per $1.00

01	Meat	33-34	Oil and gas
04	Cereal	65	Textiles
05	Fruits and vegetables	67	Iron and steel
07	Tropical products	68	Nonferrous
1	Beverages and tobacco	71	Nonelectrical machinery
4	Oils and fat	72	Electrical machinery
5	Chemicals	73	Transport equipment
26	Textile fibers	84	Clothing
28	Ore and scrap	86	Instruments, etc.
32	Coal	*	Other

Source: Charts 2 and 3.

17

TABLE 1

Comparison of Nominal Tariffs and International Price Disparities for Selected Argentine Exportables

	Tariff	Price Diff.	Draw-back	Pref. Enjoyed
Milk, powdered, dry	100	0	0	
Cheese	120	0	0.4	
Stearic acid	20	20	0	LAFTA
Pastilles	140	57	30	
Caramels	140	40	16	
Biscuits	130	20	9.4	
Orange juice, conc.	110	9	0	
Wine, red, fine	140	0	0	
Waxes, parafume	90	33.3	0	LAFTA
Tartaric acid, gran.	90	60	0.1	LAFTA
Pigments, inorganic	90	53	21.3	LAFTA
Polyethylene	100	100	0	
Polystyrene	30	50	0	
Leather, calf	90	0	1.3	
Glass, sheet	100	27	0.75	
Wire, steel, heavy	60	70	37.8	
Wire, smooth, galvanized	70	79.5	25.4	LAFTA
Wire, smooth, non-galv.	70	70	35.25	
Pipe, seamless	90	26.5	65	
Wire, barbed, galv.	90	85	25.3	
Stove, gas	130	30	0	
Wrench, fixed	80	45	15	LAFTA
Compressor	80	30	0	LAFTA
Refrigerator, household	140	23.3	0	LAFTA
Bottle-making machines	90	5	1.18	
Plow	90	30	0	LAFTA
Seed sower	90	40	0	
Automatic harvester	90	35	3.79	LAFTA
Punching machine	80	50	0	LAFTA
Lathe, parallel	90	24	0	
Press, hydraulic, 200 ton	90	25	0	
Motor, electric, 2HP	90	30	6.3	LAFTA
Coupling, 12 ton	90	27	8.25	
Gauge, electric	90	50	0	LAFTA

Source: N. A. Belozercovsky et al. "Asignación de Recursos y Exportaciones no tradicionales: Una Evaluación," (Buenos Aires: Fundación de Investigaciones Económicas Latinoamericanas, Libro FIEL No. 6, 1970).

CHART 5

Profile of Margins of Intra-LAFTA Preference:
Argentina, 1967
(weighting based on "world trade,"
i.e., total OECD imports, 1965)

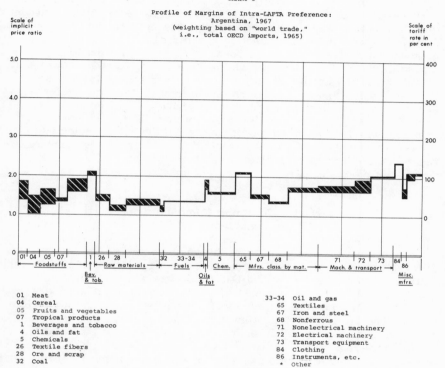

Scale of
implicit
price ratio

Scale of
tariff
rate in
per cent

01	Meat
04	Cereal
05	Fruits and vegetables
07	Tropical products
1	Beverages and tobacco
4	Oils and fat
5	Chemicals
26	Textile fibers
28	Ore and scrap
32	Coal

33-34	Oil and gas
65	Textiles
67	Iron and steel
68	Nonferrous
71	Nonelectrical machinery
72	Electrical machinery
73	Transport equipment
84	Clothing
86	Instruments, etc.
*	Other

Source: External tariffs from same sources as Chart 3. Intra-LAFTA tariffs from ALALC, Lista Consolidada de Concesiones, 1969.

19

Various weighting methods might be used in aggregating this information (e.g., in accordance with imports from LAFTA in a base year, Argentine imports from all countries, total LAFTA exports, etc.). Each method has its conceptual shortcomings. The average margins of preference indicated in Chart 5 are at least weighted consistently with the other charts, i.e., by "world trade." On the basis of this neutral criterion, Argentina had by 1969 moved about one-fifth of the way toward elimination of tariffs toward LAFTA countries. In terms of ipr's, partner countries have thus received a relative-price advantage of about 8 per cent vis-à-vis third countries in the Argentine market.* These overall averages conceal substantial differences in individual product categories. Like other countries, Argentina has made most of its concessions where it hurt least: those foodstuffs where Argentina has an absolute or comparative advantage, notably meat and grain (but not tropical products); capital goods; various raw materials; and intermediate inputs. No, or very few, preferences have been given in such sensitive categories as fuels, chemicals, textiles, automobiles, and clothing. Even the so-called complementarity agreements covering certain carefully selected items in such categories as electronic data-processing equipment, radio and television tubes, glass, and chemicals have so far affected only an infinitesimal part of the product spectrum.

The European Economic Community and Eight
Latin American Countries

Profiles of protection can be drawn up according to many different systems of classification, levels of aggregation, and weighting patterns. Depending on the availability of data and computational problems, they may take account of a variety of nontariff barriers. They may be based on a sample or on the "population" of all possible items. The profiles of Argentine import tariffs shown in Charts 2-5 were classified by the SITC because this is the easiest classification to relate to trade flows. A world-trade-weighted standard sample was used because it offered one solution to the problem of international comparability. Nontariff barriers were ignored for simplicity and because inclusion of the Argentine statistical tax on imports and of the cost of advance deposits would not have changed the picture significantly.

Charts 6-14 show in a different presentation the estimated patterns

---

*This calculation ignores the additional preferences on various products given by Argentina to Bolivia, Ecuador, Paraguay, and Uruguay.

CHART 6

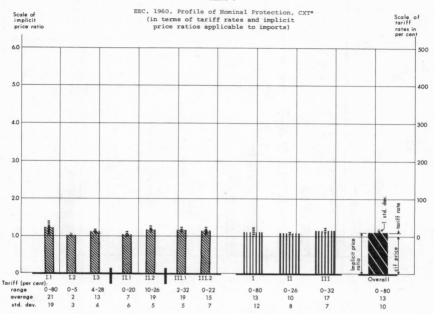

EEC, 1960, Profile of Nominal Protection, CXT*
(in terms of tariff rates and implicit
price ratios applicable to imports)

Scale of
implicit
price ratio

Scale of
tariff
rates in
per cent

Tariff (per cent):	I.1	I.2	I.3	II.1	II.2	III.1	III.2		I	II	III		Overall
range	0-80	0-5	4-28	0-20	10-26	2-32	0-22		0-80	0-26	0-32		0-80
average	21	2	13	7	19	19	15		13	10	17		13
std. dev.	19	3	4	6	5	5	7		12	8	7		10

Category I (51 products): Primary
commodities and capital goods

   1. Nonprocessed foodstuffs (13 products)
   2. Industrial raw materials (10 products)
   3. Capital goods (28 products)

Category II (43 products): Semimanufactured
and durable consumer goods

   1. Semimanufactured goods (including fuels),
     other than products of traditional
     industries (32 products)
   2. Durable consumer goods (11 products)

Category III (31 products): Current consumer
manufacturers

   1. Processed foods (14 products)
   2. Others (including semiprocessed
     products of traditional industries
     (17 products)

Overall average (125 products)

*Common external tariff (CXT), before Dillon Round concessions. The CXT was only implemented, by gradual
stages, during the 1960's. Averages and standard deviations shown for "Nonprocessed foodstuffs" (I.1)
ignore variable levies under the common agricultural policy (CAP).

    Source: Calculated from data presented by Santiago Macario in "Protectionism and Industrialization
in Latin America," Bulletin for Latin America, IX, 1 (March, 1964), Annex III.

CHART 7

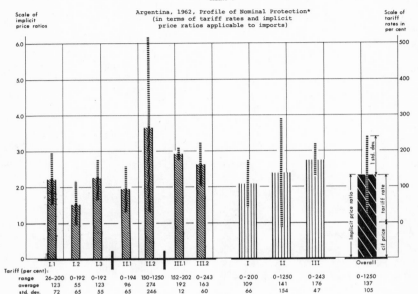

Scale of
implicit
price ratios

Argentina, 1962, Profile of Nominal Protection*
(in terms of tariff rates and implicit
price ratios applicable to imports)

Scale of
tariff
rates in
per cent

Tariff (per cent):

	I.1	I.2	I.3	II.1	II.2	III.1	III.2	I	II	III	Overall
range	26-200	0-192	0-192	0-194	150-1250	152-202	0-243	0-200	0-1250	0-243	0-1250
average	123	55	123	96	274	192	163	109	141	176	137
std. dev.	72	65	55	65	246	12	60	66	154	47	105

Category I (51 products): Primary
commodities and capital goods

   1. Nonprocessed foodstuffs (13 products)
   2. Industrial raw materials (10 products)
   3. Capital goods (28 products)

Category II (43 products): Semimanufactured
and durable consumer goods

   1. Semimanufactured goods (including fuels),
      other than products of traditional
      industries (32 products)
   2. Durable consumer goods (11 products)

Category III (31 products): Current consumer
manufactures

   1. Processed foods (14 products)
   2. Others (including semiprocessed
      products of traditional industries
      (17 products)

Overall average (125 products)

*Information brought up to date as of March, 1962. The ad valorem totals noted include ad valorem customs duties,
exchange surcharges, and rate of payment for statistical services. On the other hand, the following were not
incorporated: the 20 per cent surcharge imposed on all imports under the terms of Decree No. 8158/61 and 11260
(subsequently abolished); ad valorem equivalence of the specific duty and the various specific surcharges on
forestry and steel-making development plans. Where a product did not seem to fit into any one of the items established in the tariff, a duty of 42 per cent was assigned to it, and one of 150 per cent if it was not included in
the schedule of the exchange surcharges.

    Source: Calculated from data presented by Santiago Macario in "Protectionism and Industrialization in Latin
America," Economic Bulletin for Latin America, IX, 1 (March, 1964), Annex III.

CHART 8

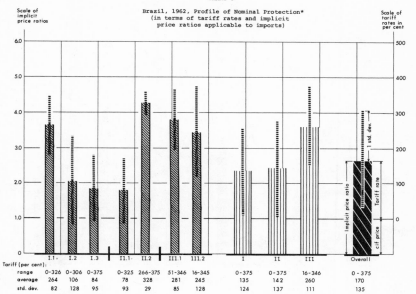

Brazil, 1962, Profile of Nominal Protection*
(in terms of tariff rates and implicit
price ratios applicable to imports)

Scale of
implicit
price ratios

Scale of
tariff
rates in
per cent

Tariff (per cent):	I.1	I.2	I.3	II.1	II.2	III.1	III.2	I	II	III	Overall
range	0-326	0-306	0-375	0-325	266-375	51-346	16-345	0-375	0-375	16-346	0-375
average	264	106	84	78	328	281	245	135	142	260	170
std. dev.	82	128	95	93	29	85	128	124	137	111	135

Category I (51 products): Primary
commodities and capital goods

1. Nonprocessed foodstuffs (13 products)
2. Industrial raw materials (10 products)
3. Capital goods (28 products)

Category II (43 products): Semimanufactured
and durable consumer goods

1. Semimanufactured goods (including fuels),
   other than products of traditional
   industries (32 products)
2. Durable consumer goods (11 products)

Category III (31 products): Current consumer
manufactures

1. Processed foods (14 products)
2. Others (including semiprocessed
   products of traditional industries
   (17 products)

Overall average (125 products)

*Information brought up to date as of March, 1962. The ad valorem total includes tariff duties; rate of customs
clearance; dues payable on improvement of port facilities and the additional cost (estimated at 200 per cent of the
cif value) of foreign exchange for goods classified in the Special Category. The following were not taken into
account: mercantile marine replacement levy; the financing of the prior deposit, of which the approximate cost is
9 per cent; consular fees, amounting to $25 for import values reaching $1,000, plus an additional $4 for every
fraction of $500 over and above that sum.

Source: Calculated from data presented by Santiago Macario in "Protectionism and Industrialization in Latin
America," Economic Bulletin for Latin America, IX, 1 (March, 1964), Annex III.

23

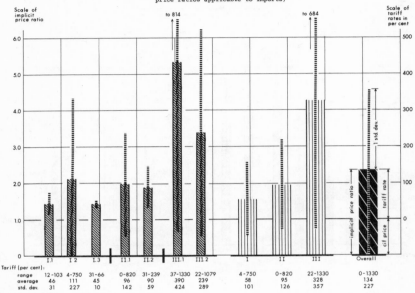

CHART 9

Chile, 1962, Profile of Nominal Protection*
(in terms of tariff rates and implicit
price ratios applicable to imports)

Tariff (per cent):

	I.1	I.2	I.3	II.1	II.2	III.1	III.2	I	II	III	Overall
range	12-103	4-750	31-66	0-820	31-239	37-1330	22-1079	4-750	0-820	22-1330	0-1330
average	46	111	45	96	90	390	239	58	95	328	134
std. dev.	31	227	10	142	59	424	289	101	126	357	227

Category I (51 products): Primary
commodities and capital goods

    1. Nonprocessed foodstuffs (13 products)
    2. Industrial raw materials (10 products)
    3. Capital goods (28 products)

Category II (43 products): Semimanufactured
and durable consumer goods

    1. Semimanufactured goods (including
       fuels) other than products of
       traditional industries (32 products)
    2. Durable consumer goods (11 products)

Category III (31 products): Current consumer
manufactures

    1. Processed foods (14 products)
    2. Others (including semiprocessed products
       of traditional industries (17 products)

Overall average (125 products)

*Information brought up to date as of June, 1962. The ad valorem total includes customs duties, tax on value of nationalized merchandise (expressed in terms of the cif ad valorem equivalent), supplementary tax, and cost of financing prior deposits; these last range from 10 to 1,000 per cent cif, which, at a rate of interest of 1.5 per cent over a period of 90 days, gives an ad valorem equivalence of 1 to 45 per cent. The consular dues of 2.5 per cent fob were not taken into account, and neither was the loading and unloading tax of $0.206 per quintal or the 3 per cent freight tax.

Source: Calculated from data presented by Santiago Macario in "Protectionism and Industrialization in Latin America," Economic Bulletin for Latin America, IX, 1 (March, 1964), Annex III.

CHART 10

Colombia, 1962, Profile of Nominal Protection*
(in terms of tariff rates and implicit
price ratios applicable to imports)

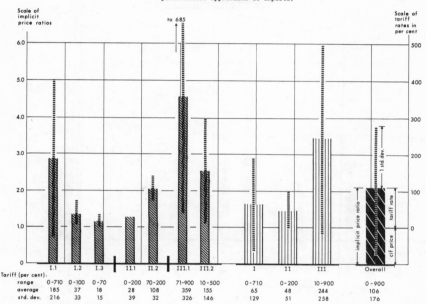

Tariff (per cent):	I.1	I.2	I.3	II.1	II.2	III.1	III.2		I	II	III		Overall
range	0-710	0-100	0-70	0-200	70-200	71-900	10-500		0-710	0-200	10-900		0-900
average	185	37	18	28	108	359	155		65	48	244		106
std. dev.	216	33	15	39	32	326	146		129	51	258		176

Category I (51 products): Primary
commodities and capital goods

    1. Nonprocessed foodstuffs (13 products)
    2. Industrial raw materials (10 products)
    3. Capital goods (28 products)

Category II (43 products): Semimanufactured
and durable consumer goods

    1. Semimanufactured goods (including
       fuels), other than products of
       traditional industries (32 products)
    2. Durable consumer goods (11 products)

Category III (31 products): Current consumer
manufactures

    1. Processed foods (14 products)
    2. Others (including semiprocessed
       products of traditional industries
       (17 products)

Overall average (125 products)

*Information brought up to date as of March, 1962. The ad valorem total noted includes customs duties, consular
dues, and development quotas. The following, on the other hand, were excluded: cost of financing the prior
deposit, since the amounts to be imposed were to come into force as from 1 September 1962; the ad valorem
equivalent of these deposits were to range from 1 to 4 per cent of the cif value.

Source: Calculated from data presented by Santiago Macario in "Protectionism and Industrialization in
Latin America," Bulletin for Latin America, IX, 1 (March, 1964), Annex III.

CHART 11

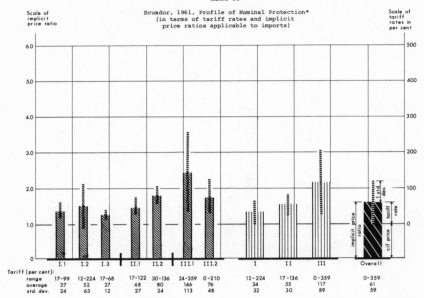

Scale of
implicit
price ratio

Ecuador, 1961, Profile of Nominal Protection*
(in terms of tariff rates and implicit
price ratios applicable to imports)

Scale of
tariff
rates in
per cent

Tariff (per cent):

	I.1	I.2	I.3	II.1	II.2	III.1	III.2	I	II	III	Overall
range	17-99	12-224	17-68	17-122	30-136	24-359	0-210	12-224	17-136	0-359	0-359
average	37	52	27	48	80	146	76	34	55	117	61
std. dev.	24	63	12	27	24	113	48	32	30	89	59

Category I (51 products): Primary
commodities and capital goods

1. Nonprocessed foodstuffs (13 products)
2. Industrial raw materials (10 products)
3. Capital goods (28 products)

Category II (43 products): Semimanufactured
and durable consumer goods

1. Semimanufactured goods (including
   fuels), other than products of
   traditional industries (32 products)
2. Durable consumer goods (11 products)

Category III (31 products): Current consumer
manufactures

1. Processed foods (14 products)
2. Others (including semiprocessed
   products of traditional industries
   (17 products)

Overall average (125 products)

*Information brought up to date as of 2 May 1961. The charges included are tariff duties, consular and harbor dues,
special duties for allocation to the southern and eastern provinces, and electrification taxes (all expressed in
ad valorem cif terms). As these duties and charges are applied on an fob basis, for conversion purposes it was
assumed that the cif value exceeded the fob value by 12 percent. The supplementary taxes of 6 per cent and 11
per cent on the cif value of products were also taken into account.

Source: Calculated from data presented by Santiago Macario in "Protectionism and Industrialization in Latin
America," Economic Bulletin for Latin America, IX, 1 (March, 1964), Annex III.

CHART 12

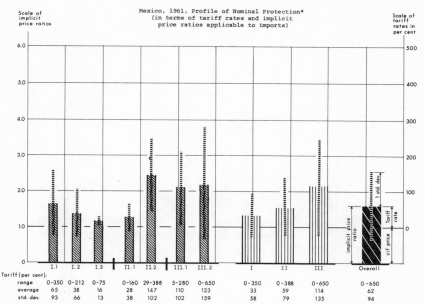

Mexico, 1961, Profile of Nominal Protection*
(in terms of tariff rates and implicit
price ratios applicable to imports)

Scale of implicit price ratios

Scale of tariff rates in per cent

Tariff (per cent):

	I.1	I.2	I.3	II.1	II.2	III.1	III.2	I	II	III	Overall
range	0-350	0-212	0-75	0-160	29-388	5-280	0-650	0-350	0-388	0-650	0-650
average	65	38	16	28	147	110	123	33	59	114	62
std. dev.	93	66	13	38	102	102	159	58	79	135	94

Category I (51 products): Primary
commodities and capital goods

1. Nonprocessed foodstuffs (13 products)
2. Industrial raw materials (10 products)
3. Capital goods (28 products)

Category II (43 products): Semimanufactured
and durable consumer goods

1. Semimanufactured goods (including
fuels) 32 products
2. Durable consumer goods (11 products)

Category III (31 products): Current consumer
manufactures

1. Processed foods (14 products)
2. Others (including semiprocessed
products of traditional insutrries
(17 products)

Overall average (125 products)

*Information brought up to date as of March, 1962. As the Mexican customs tariff is mixed in character, combining
specific and ad valorem duties, and also including an official price of each item, for the purposes of the
present study this tax structure was expressed in terms of an ad valorem total by means of the following procedure. The application of an ad valorem duty to an official price gives in practice a specific duty equivalence;
by the addition of this value to the existing specific duty a specific total can be obtained, and if this in
turn is related to the unit price, an ad valorem equivalent of the total duty will result.

Source: Calculated from data presented by Santiago Macario in "Protectionism and Industrialization in Latin
America," Bulletin for Latin America, IX, 1 (March, 1964), Annex III.

CHART 13

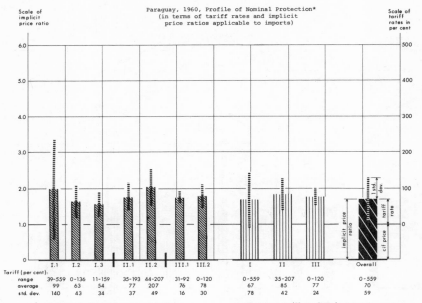

Scale of
implicit
price ratio

Paraguay, 1960, Profile of Nominal Protection*
(in terms of tariff rates and implicit
price ratios applicable to imports)

Scale of
tariff
rates in
per cent

Tariff (per cent):

	I.1	I.2	I.3	II.1	II.2	III.1	III.2	I	II	III	Overall
range	39-559	0-136	11-159	35-193	44-207	31-92	0-120	0-559	35-207	0-120	0-559
average	99	63	54	77	207	76	78	67	85	77	70
std. dev.	140	43	34	37	16	16	30	78	42	24	59

Category I (51 products): Primary
  commodities and capital goods

  1. Nonprocessed foodstuffs (13 products)
  2. Industrial raw materials (10 products)
  3. Capital goods (28 products)

Category II (43 products): Semimanufactured
  and durable consumer goods

  1. Semimanufactured goods (including fuels)
     other than products of traditional
     industries (32 products)
  2. Durable consumer goods (11 products)

Category III (31 products): Current consumer
  manufactures

  1. Processed foods (14 products)
  2. Others (including semiprocessed
     products of traditional industries
     (17 products)

Overall average (125 products)

*Up-to-date information was not available on the import regime in respect of prior deposits, sales taxes, etc.,
nor were the foreign trade yearbooks that were needed in order to obtain unit prices, which are an indispensable
requisite for expressing a specific duty in terms of its ad valorem equivalent. In the majority of cases,
therefore, it was necessary to resort to the data collected for the ECLA Secretariat study on customs duties and
other import restrictions and charges (E/CN.12/554/Add.8) and to information furnished in the course of the first
ALALC conference at Montevideo. Apart from customs duties, the following are included: exchange surcharges, sales
taxes, cost of financing prior deposit, consular dues, and stamp duties.

  Source: Calculated from data presented by Santiago Macario in "Protectionism and Industrialization in Latin
America," Economic Bulletin for Latin America, IX, 1 (March, 1964), Annex III.

CHART 14

Peru, 1960, Profile of Nominal Protection
(in terms of tariff rates and implicit
price ratios applicable to imports)

Scale of
implicit
price ratios

Scale of
tariff
rates in
per cent

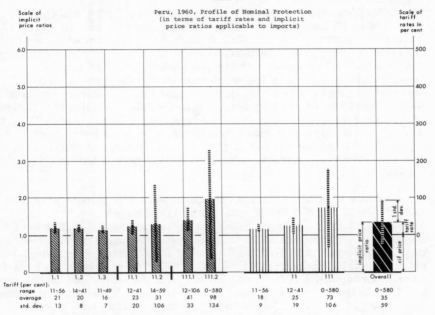

Tariff (per cent):	1.1	1.2	1.3	11.1	11.2	111.1	111.2	1	11	111	Overall
range	11-56	14-41	11-49	12-41	14-59	12-106	0-580	11-56	12-41	0-580	0-580
average	21	20	16	23	31	41	98	18	25	73	35
std. dev.	13	8	7	20	106	33	134	9	19	106	59

Category I (51 products): Primary
commodities and capital goods

   1. Nonprocessed foodstuffs (13 products)
   2. Industrial raw materials (10 products)
   3. Capital goods (28 products)

Category II (43 products): Semimanufactured and
durable consumer goods

   1. Semimanufactured goods (including fuels),
      other than products of traditional
      industries (32 products)
   2. Durable consumer goods (11 products)

Category III (31 products): Current consumer
manufactures

   1. Processed foods (14 products)
   2. Others (including semiprocessed
      products of traditional industries
      (17 products)

Overall average (125 products)

Source: Calculated from data presented by Santiago Macario in "Protectionism and Industrialization in
Latin America," Economic Bulletin for Latin America, IX, 1 (March, 1964), Annex III.

29

of nominal protection on imports, not only for the EEC and Argentina, but also for Brazil, Chile, Colombia, Ecuador, Mexico, Paraguay, and Peru. They have been drawn from data collected by the Economic Commission for Latin America, as of the early 1960's,* using an unweighted and apparently arbitrary sample of 125 items of the Brussels tariff nomenclature, aggregated in three economic categories and seven subgroups.[15] The ECLA study experimented with several different weighting and averaging techniques, each of which gave very different numerical results.**The particular series of data used in these charts appear to be the most appropriate for international comparisons and the fact that they are based on a uniform sample of well-defined and reasonably representative items permits calculation of sample standard deviations. This information is utilized in Chapter 4, in which an attempt is made to compare--internationally and over a period of time--the degree of dispersion of individual tariff rates in the respective countries, as well as the average heights of the tariffs.

At this point we comment on Charts 6-14 only to note what they indicate about the countries' patterns of tariff escalation.*** As among the seven subcategories shown in the bars on the left side of the charts, it can be seen that in most cases the relatively lowest tariffs were applied to Group I.3 (Capital Goods) and--surprisingly-- not to Group I.2 (Industrial Raw Materials). The relatively high tariffs were in Groups III.1 (Processed Foods), II.2 (Durable Consumer Goods), and III.2 (other consumer goods, notably textiles). The country whose escalation pattern was closest to the average ranking was Mexico (Spearman rank correlation: 0.94), while Chile had the most atypical (0.65). The rank correlation between the Chilean tariff structure and that of the EEC's common external tariff was only 0.1 (again based on the uniform product groupings used in Charts 6-14). Since the common external tariff was derived largely by averaging four European tariff systems, its escalation pattern can be taken as representative of that

---

*Note that the information in these charts is now ten years or so out of date and has little or no relationship to present levels of protection in most of the countries. It is nevertheless of historical interest as it reflects the situation existing when Latin American import-substitution policies at the national level were probably most extreme.

**See Table 2 in Chapter 3.

***Latin American policies with respect to tariff escalation are examined further in Chapter 6 in the section on steep escalation.

of industrial countries in general. Thus, by the tariff-escalation criterion, Chilean commercial policy was out of step by either Latin American or industrial-country standards. Other information adduced later in this study will show Chile to be an extreme case of irrational tariff-making in other respects as well.

NOTES

1. " . . . The purpose is to confine the term protection' to policies that raise domestic prices to both producers and consumers above world prices, as distinct from policies such as subsidization that raise prices only to producers." Harry G. Johnson, "Tariffs and Economic Development: Some Theoretical Issues," Journal of Development Studies, I, 1 (October, 1964), 5.

2. Jacob Viner, The Customs Union Issue (New York: Carnegie Endowment for International Peace, 1950), pp. 66-67, cited by Bela Balassa, " Tariff Protection in Industrial Countries, an Evaluation," Journal of Political Economy, LXXII, 6 (December, 1965), 573.

3. Bela Balassa and Associates, The Structure of Protection in Some Developing Countries (Baltimore: Johns Hopkins Press, 1971), Chapter 1.

4. F. D. Holzman, "Comparison of Different Forms of Trade Barriers," Review of Economics and Statistics, 51, 2 (May, 1969), 159-65.

5. See W. M. Corden, "The Structure of a Tariff System and the Effective Protective Rate," Journal of Political Economy (June, 1966), p. 223; Herbert G. Grubel and Harry G. Johnson, "Nominal Tariffs, Indirect Taxes and Effective Rates of Protection, the Common Market Countries 1959," The Economic Journal, 77 (December, 1967), passim; Balassa and Associates, op. cit., Chapter 1, pp. 7-9 Harry G. Johnson, "The Theory of Effective Protection and Preferences," Economica, XXXVI, 142 (May, 1969), 124.

6. Ian Little, Tibor Scitovsky, and Maurice Scott, Industry and Trade in Some Developing Countries: A Comparative Study (London: Oxford University Press, 1970), pp. 185-86.

7. International Monetary Fund, Annual Report on Exchange Restrictions (various issues).

8. W. M. Corden, "The Effective Protective Rate, the Uniform Tariff Equivalent and the Average Tariff," Economic Record, 42, 98 (June, 1966), 212.

9. Balassa and Associates, op. cit., Chapter 4, Tables 4.1 and 4.2.

10. Regarding the relativity of protection and the irrelevance, for most purposes, of correcting for exchange-rate overvaluation, see Little, Scitovsky, and Scott, op. cit., pp. 171-72.

11. Stephen R. Lewis, Jr., Effects of Trade Policy on Domestic Relative Prices: Pakistan, 1951-1964," American Economic Review, LVIII, 2 (March, 1968), 60-78. See also earlier articles (Lewis and Hussain, Lewis and Soligo) cited therein.

12. Paul G. Clark and Richard Weisskoff, "Import Demands and Import Policies in Brazil" (AID: mimeograph, February, 1967); Paul G. Clark, "Brazilian Import Liberalization" (Williamstown, Mass.: Center for Development Economics, Williams College, September, 1967). (Mimeograph.) Clark uses the term "effective exchange rates" instead of "implicit exchange rates," thereby risking confusion with the unrelated notion of effective protection.

13. UNCTAD, The Kennedy Round: Estimated Effects on Tariff Barriers (Geneva: United Nations Conference on Trade and Development, TD/6/Rev.1, 1968, UN Sales Number E.68.II.D.12), Chapter 2, pp. 10-19, and Annex I, pp. 44-59. (See pp. 44-45 for summary of methodology.)

14. Odd Gulbrandsen and Assar Lindbeck, "Swedish" Agricultural Policy in an International Perspective," Skandinaviska Banken Quarterly Review (1966:4), p. 95. The figure of 52 per cent implicit tariff represents an average of 41 in Benelux, 44 in France, 60 in Western Germany, and 63 in Italy. Products taken into account in the Gulbrandsen-Lindbeck estimate were wheat, sugar, milk, beef, pork, and eggs, weighted by total Western European production of the respective products.

15. Santiago Macario, "Protectionism and Industrialization in Latin America," Economic Bulletin for Latin America, IX, 1 (March, 1964), 96-101.

THE CONCEPT OF EFFECTIVE PROTECTION

In general terms,

effective protection is the protection which is given by the
entire protective structure of tariffs and quotas to a manufacturing process. The measurement takes account of the
amount by which the prices of inputs are raised by tariffs,
as well as the amount by which the price of the output is
raised: it thus seeks to estimate the amount by which the
value added, in a particular manufacturing activity, is
raised by the whole set of tariffs and quotas. More strictly,
it is the percentage amount by which value added by the
marginal unit is raised.[1]

There is nothing new in the notion that the cost-raising effect of
any customs duties levied on material inputs lowers manufacturers'
profits, offsetting the increased profits obtained from tariff protection
on the processed outputs. Those who are protectionists where finished
goods are concerned always want free trade for their raw materials.
This is reflected in the typical escalation seen in most tariff structures.
It was only in 1955, however, that the concept of the effective tariff
was formalized by a Canadian economist, Clarence L. Barber, and
the working out of its theoretical implications only began in earnest
in the mid-1960's.[2]

Just as a nominal tariff rate is, by definition, the price disparity--
i.e., domestic price less foreign price--taken as a percentage of the
foreign price of a given product, so an effective tariff rate (Z) is the
value-added disparity, i.e., domestic value added (W) less foreign
value added (V), taken as a percentage of the foreign value added in

the given process $\underline{i}$. Thus: $Z_i = \dfrac{W_i - V_i}{V_i}$. For computation purposes,

a transformed version of this formula is used: $Z_i = \dfrac{T_i - \sum_j A_{ji} T_j}{V_i}$

where T_i = nominal tariffs on outputs
$\quad\quad T_j$ = nominal tariffs on inputs
$\quad\quad A_{ji}$ = the matrix of input-output coefficients
$\quad\quad\quad$ (showing the proportion that the values
$\quad\quad\quad$ of each input bear to the values of each
$\quad\quad\quad$ output).

This transformation is only literally valid if certain assumptions are fulfilled, notably:

1. The nominal tariff rates measure the true price disparities of the respective outputs and inputs.

2. The free-of-duty foreign prices are all given, imports having infinite supply elasticity (a realistic assumption for most developing countries).

3. The input-output coefficients used are the same as would obtain in a free-trade situation and are constant.

The following example, involving only one output and one input, illustrates the computation: If half the price of cotton yarn, bearing duty at 10 per cent, consists of raw cotton that can be imported duty free and the other half is the value added by spinning, the effective tariff is 20 per cent and represents the advantage given by the protective system to spinning. If both the raw cotton and processed yarn bear a 10 per cent duty, then the effective tariff on yarn is also 10 per cent. If, however, raw cotton is subject to a 10 per cent duty while yarn has no duty, the effective protection on the yarn will be -10 per cent, representing the net disadvantage borne by yarn-processing activity as the result of the tariffs on both the output and input.* This example illustrates the important point that escalation of nominal tariffs from one stage to another of the sequence of production yields effective rates that may be much higher than the nominal rates. Backward escalation, on the other hand, can yield effective rates lower than the

---

$$*Z = \dfrac{10 - .5(0)}{.5} = 20\%$$
$$Z = \dfrac{10 - .5(10)}{.5} = 10\%$$
$$Z = \dfrac{0 - .5\,(10)}{.5} = -10\%$$

corresponding nominal rates or even negative effective rates. This happens frequently in Latin American tariffs. Thus, Argentina levies a 30 per cent duty on wood pulp, but does not protect newsprint.*

SOME METHODOLOGICAL PROBLEMS

The principal purpose of investigating effective protection is to evaluate the entire protective structure of a country. Since it would be impractical to aggregate estimates for each individual activity, most empirical researchers use broad industrial averages, getting their information on input coefficients and on value added from inter-industry input-output tables. This has given rise, however, to serious statistical and theoretical problems. Attempts to resolve these problems, through refinement of the definition of effective tariffs, have generated much esoteric debate in the professional economic journals.

One of the methodological problems is that of whether and how to take account of protective effects with respect to inputs not traded internationally (e.g., electricity, services, etc.). The so-called Balassa method treats nontraded inputs like other inputs and assumes their prices contain no protection. The Corden method includes the nontraded inputs in value added. Calculations based on the former give substantially higher effective rates than the latter, so this question is of real importance for empirical work.[3]

Fundamental problems arise when one drops the assumption that input-output coefficients are fixed and tries to take account of the substitution effects whereby, in a highly protectionist economy, rela-tively highly priced material inputs are partly replaced by inputs of primary factors (labor). For this and other reasons, estimates of effective protection based on the domestic input-output table will be different from those based on import coefficients under hypothetical free trade. In any case, the latter estimates are obviously not directly observable and usually have to be made on the basis of domestic coef-ficients, which give rise to much bias, or of the coefficients given by input-output tables of more liberal countries. Various ways around these problems have been proposed, but there is little agreement and certainly no easy answer.[4]

---

*Many other examples can be found of negative effective protection in the tariff schedules, but in many cases ad hoc exemptions from tariffs on input are given to favored processing firms, possibly more for political than for deliberate commercial-policy reasons.

There are also algebraic anomalies in the measurement of effective protection. The definitional formula $Z = (W-V)/V$ is not a well-behaved function. When value added at world prices is close to zero, the calculated effective tariff swings abruptly from plus infinity to minus infinity, giving what appear to be nonsense results. In any case, all very extreme values--such as 5,000 per cent effective protection, plus or minus-- have no quantitative meaning.[5] What such results probably mean substantively is that the country in question is making poor use of its resources: the value added by the given productive process is neglible when measured in world prices. Alternatively, it may simply mean that the input-output coefficients used in calculation were grossly in error.

Particularly interesting are those cases in which, when values of all inputs and outputs are deflated from domestic prices to the prices that would prevail under free trade, the processing activity in a highly protectionist country shows negative value added. This implies that, even though the individual producer may have made money, as far as the country is concerned such production was worse than useless. Resources worth valuable foreign exchange were turned into final products that were worth less after processing than the materials used up in making them. In an article that attracted much attention, Ronald Soligo and Joseph J. Stern[6] found such results in 23 out of 48 Pakistani industries studied. This seemed to be a frightening result, but a subsequent article by P. T. Ellsworth[7] indicated that many of these cases of negative value added were spurious and could be attributed to the too-easy assumption that, since there appeared to be excess demand throughout the economy, the implicit price ratios indicated by the tariff schedule really reflected true disparities between domestic and foreign prices. In reality, however, part of the tariff on output was unutilized. Using too large a deflator to convert domestic output prices to free-trade prices makes value added at free-trade prices appear to be negative when the process uses a high proportion of material inputs (e.g., in assembly operations) and when such inputs are subject to little or no protection. In his estimates of effective protection in the United States, G. Basevi had simply thrown out cases of negative value added as mathematically absurd. Some of the more recent studies, however, while recognizing that many apparent cases of negative value added are spurious or are difficult to interpret, have concluded that the criterion does help identify wasteful production and is therefore useful for project evaluation.[8]

EFFECTIVE TARIFF RATES, IMPLICIT VALUE
ADDED RATIOS, AND EXCHANGE RATES

It has been seen that nominal protection can be expressed either as a nominal tariff rate or as a price ratio (or, more frequently, the

implicit price ratio) between domestic and foreign prices and that for
many purposes the latter is the more convenient expression.

The same is true with effective protection, except that here we
are dealing with ratios involving a special kind of price, the price of
value added.[9] If the rate of effective protection is the difference
between the price of value added under protection and that under free
trade, taken as a percentage of the latter, i.e., $Z = (W-V)/V \times 100$,
one can define a value added ratio (or implicit value added ratio--
ivar), i.e., $1 + Z = W/Z$. Miguel A. Almada and Hector L. Diéguez
have shown that use of this expression, which they call the coefficient
of effective protection, is more suited than the effective tariff rate (Z)
for analyzing combined protective and exchange-rate effects.[10] Also,
it lends itself to international and intertemporal comparisons of structures of protection when one is mainly concerned with the relative
treatment accorded to various traded goods (commercial policy).
Only when one is concerned with the competitiveness of traded goods
vs. domestic goods (balance-of-payments policy) is it necessary to
adjust for overvaluation of the currency, by calculation of net effective
rates (corresponding to the net nominal rates already discussed).

The theoretical literature on the interaction of exchange rates
and rates of protection, when intermediate goods and interindustry
relationships are taken into account, is too esoteric to review here.[11]
Attention may be called, however, to a concept which, for effective
protection, is the straightforward counterpart of the implicit exchange
rates already illustrated in Chart 5. This is the exchange rate necessary for the rate of effective protection on value added to be zero.[12]
It is used for evaluation of new projects in relation to comparative
advantage, showing the exchange rates that would have to prevail
before various industries became fully competitive. In some cases
(those where value added at free-trade prices is actually negative),
there may be no rate of exchange at which production is justified on
economic grounds.

COMPARISON OF PROFILES OF NOMINAL
AND EFFECTIVE PROTECTION:
PREREFORM ARGENTINA

Chart 15, based on calculations by Balassa,[13] is convenient for
an illustrative comparison of nominal and effective protection because
the nominal tariff data used are apparently taken from the same
source[14] as the data underlying the averages shown in Chart 2.

Since calculation of effective tariffs requires input-output information, Bela Balassa classified his 24 industries according to an

CHART 15

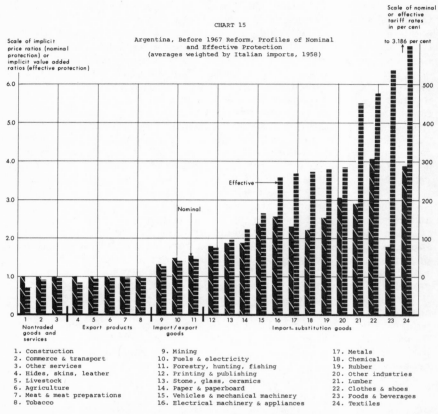

Scale of implicit
price ratios (nominal
protection) or
implicit value added
ratios (effective protection)

Argentina, Before 1967 Reform, Profiles of Nominal
and Effective Protection
(averages weighted by Italian imports, 1958)

Scale of nominal
or effective
tariff rates
in per cent

to 3.186 per cent

1. Construction
2. Commerce & transport
3. Other services
4. Hides, skins, leather
5. Livestock
6. Agriculture
7. Meat & meat preparations
8. Tobacco

9. Mining
10. Fuels & electricity
11. Forestry, hunting, fishing
12. Printing & publishing
13. Stone, glass, ceramics
14. Paper & paperboard
15. Vehicles & mechanical machinery
16. Electrical machinery & appliances

17. Metals
18. Chemicals
19. Rubber
20. Other industries
21. Lumber
22. Clothes & shoes
23. Foods & beverages
24. Textiles

Sources: Based on estimates by Bela Balassa, "Resource Allocation and Economic Integration in Latin
America" (April, 1966); Nomenclatura Arencelaria y Recargos de Importacion, 1965; and Input-output table
for 1958.

38

input-output matrix relating to the year 1958. In addition to industries producing tradables, three industries from the purely domestic sector (construction, commerce and transport, and other services) are shown. Although their nominal protection is zero (by definition), they are affected by negative effective protection. In the traditional Argentine export industries (numbers 4-8), Balassa ignored the import tariffs, which are obviously all redundant. He likewise ignored the negative nominal protection implied by the export retentions of up to 25 per cent (imposed by Decree-Law 5, 168 of 1958 but largely eliminated by 1964), so that the nominal tariff in the export industries is also shown as zero. As for industries producing both exports and import-competing goods, Balassa's nominal tariffs are sales-weighted averages of zero for the export portion and of the scheduled tariffs for the import-competing portion. Within the industry categories of the import-substitution sector, Balassa had used two alternative weighting principles: unweighted arithmetic averages and Italian 1958 import weights. The two methods, each of which avoids the own-trade-weighting bias (discussed in Chapter 3), give different absolute results, especially for effective rates. In Chart 15, there are shown only the averages obtained by the Italian trade weights, which correspond better, conceptually, to the OECD-trade weights used for Chart 2.

A word of caution should be introduced at this point regarding the lack of literal accuracy in the effective-protection estimates depicted in Chart 15. They should be taken only as a very simplified illustration of how the effective-tariff calculation would work out, using the Balassa method of treating nontraded inputs and accepting a number of assumptions which were probably not literally fulfilled at any particular historical time. One of the more serious departures from reality is that apparently no account was taken of the fact that, from 1958 until the tariff reform of 1967, more than 50 per cent of Argentine imports were exempt from surcharges by virture of special ad hoc exemptions. Such exemptions, applying especially to capital goods but also to many current inputs, would reduce the averages of nominal protection and increase the levels of effective protection.

On Chart 15 the industries producing tradable goods have been arranged according to the relative rank of their computed effective protection. It will be noted that negative effective tariff rates (implicit-value-added ratios of less than unity) are shown for nontraded goods and services and for export products. This reflects the cost disadvantage resulting from positive nominal protection on these industries' inputs, which are not compensated by any nominal protection on output. Industries whose products are both imported and exported and the first four import-substitution industries show effective protection at about the same levels as their nominal protection. This suggests that, by and large, their inputs and outputs bore about the same incidence

of nominal protection. Beginning with Industry 15 (vehicles and
mechanical machinery), effective protection is substantially higher
than nominal protection. This illustrates the well-known property of
effective protection: escalation of nominal protection at various stages
of processing tends to be greatly magnified in the escalation of effective
protection, especially in industries making finished consumer goods.
The extremely high effective tariff rate of over 3,000 per cent shown
for textiles (Industry 24) was undoubtedly grossly overestimated,
possibly as a result of anomalies in the Italian trade-weight pattern.
Nevertheless, even the unweighted average was still over 1,000 per
cent, showing that Argentina shared the universal propensity to give
priority to import substitution in this industry. Since textiles are an
input to clothing, the higher nominal protection shown in clothing and
shoes than in textiles, did not yield as high effective protection.

When industries are rank-ordered on an ascending scale of
effective protection, as in Chart 15, the profile not only summarizes
information about the protective structure, it also "tells us the direction
in which this structure causes resources to be pulled as between
activities producing traded goods. Domestic production will shift
from low to high effective-protective-rate activities."[15] However,
consumption will shift from final goods with high nominal tariffs
toward goods with low nominal tariffs. Therefore, one should consider
the rank-ordering in terms of nominal protection as well as in terms
of effective protection.

Under certain assumptions regarding constant costs and competitive markets for products and factors of production in the domestic
economy, ranking by effective rates of protection may also provide
a ranking by comparative advantage. (See below, "Relationship
Between Comparative Advantage and Profiles of Protection," Chapter 5.)
In Latin America, however, it is unlikely that these conditions will be
fulfilled. Therefore, while estimates of effective protection may give
some indications of the pattern of comparative advantage in a country,
they may also be misleading in greater or lesser degree. In any case,
depending on the statistical dependability of the tariff averages, the
input-output coefficients, and so forth, a rank-ordered scale of protection such as is given in Chart 15 can be a useful aid in the evaluation
of industrialization policy.

NOTES

1. Ian Little, Tibor Scitovsky, and Maurice Scott, Industry and Trade in Some Developing Countries: A Comparative Study (London: Oxford University Press, 1970), p. 169.

2. Among the pioneering contributions were:
Clarence L. Barber, "The Canadian Tariff Policy," Canadian Journal of Economics and Political Science, 21 (November, 1955), 513-30; Swedish Customs Tariff Commission, Revision of the Swedish Customs Tariff (Stockholm, 1957); W. M. Corden, "The Tariff" in A. Hunter, ed., The Economics of Australian Industry (Melbourne: Melbourne University Press, 1963), pp. 162-63; Santiago Macario, "Protectionism and Industrialisation in Latin America Economic Bulletin for Latin America, IX, 1 (March, 1964), 61-101; Harry G. Johnson, "The Theory of Tariff Structure with Special Reference to World Trade and Development," Trade and Development (Geneva: Institut Universitaire de Hautes Etudes Internationales, 1965); Bela Balassa, "Tariff Protection in Industrial Countries: An Evaluation, Journal of Political Economy, LXXII, 6 (December, 1965), 73-94; and G. Basevi, "The United States Tariff Structure: Estimates of Effective Rates of Protection of U.S. Industries and Industrial Labor," Review of Economics and Statistics, XLVIII (1966), 147-60.

3. For a discussion, see W. M. Corden, The Structure of a Tariff System and the Effective Protective Rate," Journal of Political Economy (June, 1966), pp. 226-28. Bela Balassa and Associates. Structure of Protection in Some Developing Countries (Baltimore: Johns Hopkins Press, 1971), Chapter 1; Little, Scitovsky, and Scott, op. cit., pp. 169-71.

4. Cf. Corden, op. cit., pp. 233-36; Balassa and Associates, op. cit., Chapter 1: Little, Scitovsky, and Scott, op. cit., pp. 172-74; J. Clark Leith, "Substitution and Supply Elasticities in Calculating the Effective Protective Rate," Quarterly Journal of Economics, 82, 4 (November, 1968), 588-601; James Anderson and Seiji Naya, "Substitution and Two Concepts of the Effective Rate of Protection," American Economic Review, LIX, 4, Part 1 (September, 1969), 607-12; J. M. Finger, "Substitution and the Effective Rate of Protection," Journal of Political Economy, LXXVII, 6 (1969), 972-75.

5. Little, Scitovsky, and Scott, op. cit., pp. 173-74; Balassa and Associates, op. cit., Appendix to Chapter 1.

6. Ronald Soligo and Joseph J. Stern, "Tariff Protection, Import Substitution, and Investment Efficiency," Pakistan Development Review (Summer, 1965), pp. 249-70.

7. P. T. Ellsworth, "Import Substitution in Pakistan--A Comment," Research Paper #9, University of Wisconsin (June, 1966).

8. "Negative value added at world prices is not necessarily caused by an unusual degree of inefficiency, although it can be, but is most likely to occur where there is 'over' production of goods that are uneconomical from the standpoint of opportunity costs." Stephen E. Guisinger, "Negative Value Added and the Theory of Effective Protection," Quarterly Journal of Economics, 83, 3 (August, 1969), 415-33. See also Balassa and Associates, op. cit., Chapter 1. On the other hand, Augustine H. H. Tan, "Differential Tariffs, Negative Value-Added and the Theory of Effective Protection, " American Economic Review, LX, 1 (March, 1970), 107-15, has shown several situations in general equilibrium analysis where the existence of negative value added tells nothing about whether or not an industry would be viable without protection. Thus, the opinion of economic theorists on this subject is still in a state of flux.

9. One of the difficulties with intuitive comprehension of effective protection is that the ratio of the price of value added is ill-defined. It has no natural unity, being composed of the weighted sum of the contributions of primary factors to a unit of product. It is usually derived as a net residual in input-output tables or in industrial censuses. See W. P. Travis, "The Effective Rate of Protection and the Question of Labor Protection in the United States," Journal of Political Economy, (May-June, 1968), pp. 443-61.

10. Miguel A. Almada and Hector L. Diéguez, Protección Efectiva y Tipo de Cambio (Buenos Aires: Instituto Torcuato di Tella, Centro de Investigaciones Económicas, December, 1968). pp. 25-26.

11. See, for example, W. M. Corden, "Effective Protective Rates in the General Equilibrium Model: A Geometric Note," Oxford Economic Papers, 21, 2 (July, 1969), 135-41.

12. Stephen R. Lewis and Stephen E. Guisinger, "Measuring Protection in a Developing Country: The Case of Pakistan," Journal of Political Economy, LXXVI, 6 (November-December, 1968), 186-90.

13. Bela Balassa, "Resource Allocation and Economic Integration in Latin America'' (Conference at Cornell University on ''The Next Decade of Latin American Development," April 20-22, 1966) (mimeograph--revised), Table 2.

14. Comisión de Aranceles de la República Argentina, Nomenclatura Arancelaria y Recargos de Importación 1965 (Buenos Aires: Ministerio de Economía, 1965).

15. Corden, "The Structure of a Tariff System and the Effective Protective Rate," op. cit., p. 224, Corden's View on the usefulness of the effective protection concept as a guide to the direction of resource-pull in the economy has been challenged by Tan, op. cit.,pp. 113-16.

Customs duties and export subsidies are legally expressed in quantitative terms; both customs duties and nontariff barriers have effects on relative prices and the terms of trade that are quantifiable and, in principle, measurable. Nevertheless, empirical measurement of levels of protection, even in the simplest form of nominal tariff averages, has presented so many conceptual and practical problems that, more than 40 years after the League of Nations' pioneer attempts to prepare tariff indices,[1] there still exists no authoritative source of internationally comparable statistics on protection.

WHAT IS BEING MEASURED?

Much of the problem has reflected confusion about what one is trying to measure. It is not primarily the revenue yield of a tariff, or an estimate of the amount of potential trade frustrated by a tariff, or the tariff's impact on the balance of payments. Now that protection is defined primarily in terms of international price disparities, it is more clear that what are involved are price-index numbers. But they are price indexes of a special kind, i.e., sets of averages of price (or price-disparity) relatives based, not on the prices prevailing in a reference year (as in a wholesale-price index), but on the prices that would prevail at any given time in the absence of protection. The main desideratum of such indices is that they lend themselves to international as well as intertemporal comparisons. Furthermore, point estimates of an absolute overall index of the level of protection are of less interest than the relative levels shown for economically meaningful categories and subcategories. The degree of dispersion of levels of protection within categories is as relevant as the variation among categories. Finally, it is important to have protection indices for exports as well as for imports.

44

CLASSIFICATION PROBLEMS

A major difficulty in averaging protective levels arises from the fact that no single system of classification is meaningful for all purposes. Most countries, including many in Latin America, now base their tariffs on some version of the Brussels tariff nomenclature (BTN). It is an excellent classification for the practical use of customs officials, but its higher levels of aggregation are useless for economic analysis, while at the detailed levels (under four digits) each country's system is different and may involve from 5,000 to 10,000 distinctly defined items. Fortunately, there is one-for-one correspondence at the four-digit level of the BTN with the four- and five-digit level of the Standard International Trade Classification, in which most countries now report trade statistics on a more or less comparable basis. Also, concordances exist permitting translation from SITC into a number of other standard systems of classification. There are thus important advantages to articulating tariff averages and other indices of nominal protection in terms of the SITC. Where countries do not use a customs classification having a systematic correspondence with SITC, or where ad hoc classifications used for, say, multiple exchange rates do not correspond to the national customs nomenclature, reconciliation of product classifications presents very great problems.

Although it is fairly easy to regroup disaggregated SITC data into input-output industrial classifications, one cannot conveniently reclassify the latter in terms consistent with trade statistics or customs tariffs. This raises a problem in studies of effective protection, which usually have to be based on input-output matrices. Industries and sectors as defined for input-output purposes are either too aggregative or, when taken from a very disaggregated matrix, say 200 x 200, the industry definitions still may not reconcile with product definitions.

In addition to having industrial and sectoral classifications consistent with input-output data, it is also of interest to classify indices of levels of protection in accordance with other economic criteria suitable for the purpose at hand.* A special type of product cross-classification is UNCTAD's identification of "products-of-interest

---

*Among the more useful economic classifications are the following:

1. Three-way classification by primary commodities, semi-manufactures, and manufactures. See UNCTAD, TD/B/C.2/3, July 2, 1965.   (continued)

to developing countries," used in the UNCTAD study of the Kennedy
Round to illustrate the tendency for the tariff structures of industrial
countries to discriminate against products of developing countries.

WEIGHTING

Being a form of price index, tariff averaging is subject to the
index-number problem with respect to weighting. Tariff averages
weighted by imports of the country being studied may measure the
revenue yield of the tariff but they cannot measure protection. As is
well known, such own-trade-weighted averages are biased downwards,
since prohibitive duties are, by definition, excluded from the average.
This particular bias can be avoided by taking so-called unweighted
averages of all the nomenclature positions in the various sections of
the tariff, but this really involves weighting according to an irrelevant,
fortuitous, and internationally noncomparable criterion: the fineness
of nomenclatural subdivisions in the particular tariff document. The
tariff for an item important in a country's trade, like passenger automobiles, will get the same weight as the tariff for a minor item, like
spark plugs. Another problem with unweighted tariff averages is that
they are often biased upwards by the presence of a few extremely high
tariffs of little economic significance. The solution of the weighting
dilemma is sometimes sought in a combination of these two methods.

A good illustration of the divergent estimates obtained by own-
trade weighting and by two methods of arithmetic averaging of tariff
positions is shown in Table 2, prepared by the Economic Commission
for Latin America (ECLA).

Column 1 shows averages for a sample representing at least
85 per cent of total trade, where weighting was based on own imports.
It obviously under-weights high-tariff items, except in durable consumer
goods. Figures in Column 2 are simple arithmetic means for the
same 85 per cent sample. Since goods imported in small amounts or
not at all are excluded, this method is also biased downward in most
groupings shown. Column 3 shows simple arithmetic means of all
BTN items in the respective tariffs, weighted only by the frequency

---

(Continued)
    2. "Broad economic categories," proposed by UN Statistical
Commission, E/CN.3/341, April 8, 1966.

    3. EEC's "Noyaux de regroupement," Bureau Statistique des
Communautées Europaennes, Classification Statistique et Tarifaire.

TABLE 2

Comparison of Average Levels of Incidence of Import Duties
and Charges in Argentina, Brazil, Chile, and France
(weighted averages and simple arithmetic means)

Category and group	Argentina I	Argentina II	Argentina III	Brazil I	Brazil II	Brazil III	Chile I	Chile II	Chile III	France III
Category I. Primary commodities	18.5	54.2	131	2.9	13.4	40	20.2	40.8	93	
1. Unprocessed foodstuffs	40.6	40.4	145	1.1	9.5	43	14.2	33.5	114	21
2. Raw materials	42.7	65.0	129	22.0	19.7	38	16.1	45.1	86	5
3. Unprocessed fuels	1.0	6.9	34	0.8	10.2	29	34.1	53.5	30	1
Category II. Durable, intermediate and capital goods	64.7	96.9	138	36.9	40.8	45	39.6	45.9	67	
1. Intermediate products	49.6	62.1	138	26.1	31.0	43	40.6	45.3	73	17
2. Processed fuels	1.2	4.0	95	22.8	29.3	30	40.1	45.5	89	7
3. Capital goods	78.2	84.7	130	45.6	46.1	45	37.3	40.5	44	19
4. Durable consumer goods	699.7	612.2	181	79.1	60.0	75	83.7	83.4	104	24
Category III. Current consumer manufactures	66.5	110.0	175	40.4	50.4	87	56.8	66.2	126	
1. Processed foodstuffs and tobacco	142.4	136.4	180	50.5	56.3	91	62.8	126.4	188	25
2. Chemical and pharmaceutical products	62.9	102.7	151	35.4	25.0	69	14.7	16.5	82	20
3. Other current consumer goods	63.6	108.6	175	37.3	52.0	88	55.1	64.5	118	19
Overall total	52.7	91.5	151	28.8	40.1	60	38.2	49.2	93	18

Source: Santiago Macario, "Protectionism and Industrialization in Latin America," Economic Bulletin for Latin America, IX, 1 (March, 1964), 73.

distribution of numbers of items in each category. Given the large
number of items of insignificant intrinsic importance bearing high
duties, these estimates are probably biased upwards, except--again--
in the case of durable consumer goods. In view of the a priori reasons
for believing Columns 1 and 2 to be underestimates of the true averages
and Column 3 to be overestimated, a series of data intermediate
between 2 and 3 can be considered to reflect more accurate orders of
magnitude. The averages shown for Argentina in Chart 7 (based on
other information in the same ECLA study) meet this criterion. Also,
since the same 125-item sample was used for the other countries
shown in Charts 7-14, while the three other methods have weightings
that are not internationally identical, it would also appear that this
method gives the best results for the whole group of countries.*

  Another weighting method, used when calculating effective tariffs
by domestic input coefficients, is to weight each industry by domestic
supply deflated to world prices (to measure nominal protection) and
by domestic value added deflated to world value added (to measure
effective protection). This method is not free of substitution effects,
however, and sales data are unlikely to be available in the required
detail. Weighting by either domestic supply or domestic value without
deflation to world prices is, of course, likely to result in overestimation
of nominal protection, since it involves including the tariffs themselves
in the weights.

  Because no one knows what the composition of a country's imports
or its total supply would be in the absence of protection, many researchers have chosen to weight indices of levels of protection by
some neutral standard, external to the country under study. In Latin
America, for example, one might use the total pattern of trade of the
LAFTA countries. This has the disadvantage that many Latin American
countries have parallel import substitution policies, which abnormally
penalize imports, for example, of consumer durables and other finished
consumer goods, and abnormally encourage imports of capital goods.
Therefore, the common substitution effects of broadly similar commercial policies will still distort the weighting pattern from what it
would be under free trade, giving too little emphasis to automobiles
(high protection) and too much to machinery (low protection). Nevertheless, weighting by total LAFTA imports would still be a neutral
standard for comparing individual countries in the area.

----

  *The figures shown for Brazil and Chile in Table 2 disregard
Brazilian multiple exchange rates and certain supplementary charges
applied by Chile. These are included in the data underlying Charts
8 and 9.

Balassa's use of Italian import weights in the calculations underlying Chart 15 has already been mentioned. He chose Italy as being the European country most comparable to Argentina. The shortcoming here was that Italy's own trade pattern in 1958 was itself highly distorted by protection and other special circumstances, although to a much lesser extent than was that of Argentina.

The most neutral of all systems for weighting imports is one in which the whole world market (or a proxy) is taken as a weighting standard against which to compare tariffs of an individual country with another. The closest proxy to world production (or consumption) for which data are conveniently available in consistent SITC classifications is the total import trade of the industrial countries. Distortions resulting from national protective structures are assumed largely to cancel out, especially as much of the total recorded trade of OECD countries reflects intratrade of preferential groupings or imports of low-tariff countries. Balassa and Associates have used such a proxy for world trade in averaging nominal tariffs and effective tariffs based on free-trade input-output coefficients.[2] Under the four-digit level of SITC, however, they used own-trade weighting of the countries under study. The UNCTAD study of the Kennedy Round used a two-stage proportional-probability sampling system where the sample items were first randomly drawn in accordance with probabilities weighted by total OECD imports. Probabilities for the second stage (under SITC four-digits) were weighted in accordance with finer commodity breakdowns available for U.S. and EEC trade. Since the definition of protection is in terms of disparities of domestic prices from world prices, the use of world-trade weights is a type of Laspeyre index-number formula (weighting in terms of total domestic sales or domestic value added--deflated--would correspond to a Paasche formula). The main justification for world-trade weighting, however, is that it is politically neutral for international comparisons and that it is simply the most convenient way of giving greater weight to automobiles than to spark plugs without using own-trade weighting. Subcategory averages obtained by world-trade weighting can then be reaggregated in accordance with any system one wishes, including own-trade weighting, without danger of bias from exclusion of high-tariff items.

SAMPLING

Sampling recommends itself for measurement of protection just as for any other market-basket type of price index. Following are the advantages:

1. It is more convenient and less costly than measuring the entire population of thousands of items with differentiated tariff rates.

2. More information can be collected on each sample item than could otherwise be taken systematically into account, e.g., existence of nontariff barriers.

3. A precise market basket of items can be defined, ensuring international comparability if a neutral weighting system has been used.

4. Individual items can be defined as precisely as necessary to permit their regrouping in any reclassification required - BTN, SITC, broad economic groupings, input-output, etc. - thus solving much of the problem of reconciling nomenclatures.

5. Information on the variance of the population need not be lost through the successive averaging that is usually involved when making international comparisons from data on the whole population of possible products.

The disadvantage of sampling is the inevitable loss of precision in estimating averages. Because of the very high variance of tariffs, especially in Latin America, considerable imprecision is to be expected. This can be reduced by good sample design, design employing stratification, proportional probability sampling, and randomization. This permits use of statistical "t"-tests, etc., to evaluate the level of precision obtained. The representativeness of the sample can also be evaluated by comparing results with estimates obtained by other methods. Such tests made of the UNCTAD 504-item sample used in the Kennedy Round study indicated that, for tariffs of industrial countries, it was a satisfactory predictor of results obtained by full count of the population.[3]

As the first step toward consideration of a common external tariff with a view toward eventual transformation of the Latin American Free Trade Association into a customs union, the LAFTA Secretariat collected in 1968 a sample of 300-plus products to be used in comparing tariff structures of the 11 member countries.[4] This sample was apparently constructed according to an approach entirely different from that of the UNCTAD sample. There were no attempts to represent the entire gamut of import trade, to weight the relative trade importance of the products, to use stratification or randomization as means of ensuring the representativeness of the sample, or to reconcile the product identifications in terms of both the BTN and the SITC. The sampled products were selected, with computation of effective protection in mind, so as to provide a number of full input-to-output sequences (i.e., from raw materials through intermediate products to final products). Various branches of the food, metals and metal-fabricating, chemical, and textile industries are well represented.

On the other hand, there is no representation whatsoever of some of the most interesting sectors, viz., grains and flour, mineral fuels, wood and paper, electrical equipment (other than household durables), and transport equipment.

Despite these methodological drawbacks, the data obtained from the 11 participating governments constitute the best source of relatively up-to-date information for use in international comparisons of the national protective structures in Latin America. Great effort must have been expended by the LAFTA Secretariat and the reporting countries in converting the predominantly specific or mixed Latin American tariffs into comparable ad valorem terms, in making the fob-cif adjustments, in adjusting for special charges and multiple exchange rates, and in coping with a host of nomenclatural problems.

Partly as a cross-check on the representativeness of the UNCTAD sample and partly as a means of evaluating the gaps in the coverage of the LAFTA sample, the author has made a direct comparison of the results obtained by the two methods. This required reclassifying the LAFTA sample into SITC terms and weighting it on a world-trade-weights basis similar to that used for Charts 1 through 5. Despite the considerable differences in sampling methods, there was found to be a remarkably close correspondence between the two sets of estimates of Argentine postreform levels of protection for comparable product categories.

ADJUSTMENT OF TARIFF-RATE DATA

Systematic evaluation of protection requires that import tariffs be shown uniformly in cif ad valorem terms and export duties and subsidies in fob ad valorem terms. However, all the LAFTA countries except Argentina, Brazil, and Columbia still apply specific or mixed duties.[5] LAFTA Resolution No. 122 (V) recommended that all member countries adopt the ad valorem system, and Resolution No. 133 (V) similarly recommended adoption of the Brussels principles of customs valuation, but neither resolution imposed a deadline.

Therefore, in order to know what the tariff levels really are in most LAFTA countries, it is necessary to make item-by-item conversions of specific and mixed duties into ad valorem percentages. There are three principal sources of price information for this recalculation. One would involve taking import prices directly from trade invoices. This is not practical for private researchers, and it is usually not even feasible for a government statistical office. Secondly, one can use unit values from the trade statistics. However, these are often misleading sources of average import prices, because the level

of aggregation in trade statistics is usually higher than that in the
tariff classifications, because qualitative differences are concealed
in the unit values, and because the country concerned may not even
import a given item. for which it is desired to know the ad valorem
tariff. (A partial solution to this last problem is to use import unit
values of a nearby country or export unit values--corrected to cif--
reported by a major world supplier.[6] The third possibility is to use
outside information, such as quotations found in international price
bulletins for certain standardized items, adjusting for estimated
average freight. One variation of the third method is to use the pre-
scribed arbitrary price appraisals (aforos) laid down by some countries
in order to ensure that duty gets paid on at least a certain minimum
valuation. The LAFTA Secretariat has selected as its standard the
official prices shown in the Mexican tariff schedule. To these are
added 20 per cent for an approximate conversion from fob to cif. For
the landlocked countries, Bolivia and Paraguay, the fob-cif adjustment
is 25 per cent.

Most other adjustments of customs-duty data to include or exclude
the various surcharges and special taxes are reasonably straightforward, but laborious to carry out, especially when working from the
population of tariff rates. This is a strong argument for using a
sample.

As mentioned, the cost of prior deposits is taken into account
in terms of the cost of credit (usually 2-3 per cent per month).

The treatment of preferential rates raises interesting questions.
In order to evaluate the margin of intra-LAFTA preference, both
most-favored-nation (MFN) and preferential tariff structures should
be measured. However, in the early stages of tariff dismantlement,
the preferential cuts are unlikely to be sufficient to make beneficiary
partner countries competitive against third countries. Where the
preferential countries are able to compete to a limited extent, but,
because of supply inelasticity within the LAFTA zone, third countries
are still the marginal suppliers, the level of nominal protection in
price terms will still be determined by the MFN tariffs. At some
stage, however, undercutting of third-country price quotations will
presumably occur for a number of products in intrazonal trade, and
from that time on the preferential tariff may determine the true levels
of nominal and effective protection. Judging by the commodity categories in which Argentina has made its intra-LAFTA tariff concessions
to date, one can fairly safely assume that the preferences shown in
Chart 5 have not yet significantly affected the true levels of nominal
or effective protection.

DIRECT PRICE COMPARISONS

The definition of nominal protection refers not to the legal customs duties in the tariff schedules but to the international price disparities associated with these and other protective measures. The implicit price ratios estimated from the legal rates are only a proxy for the true price ratios, from which they may diverge substantially because of redundancy in the legal tariff or because of price effects of non-tariff barriers prevailing over the effects of the legal tariff.*

Direct price-comparison estimates are not only difficult to obtain, but they are themselves also subject to serious errors of observation. A major source of error in the case of differentiated goods is difference in product quality of the imported versus the domestic commodity; this usually results in underestimation of nominal protection, where developing countries are concerned.[7] Moreover, in making direct comparisons it is important to use the domestic price quotation that is most comparable to the cif import price, i.e., the factory price. This differs from the user price, which includes wholesale and retail markups and domestic transport costs. The combined effect of such errors of price observation may be quite high in Latin American countries.

In view of these problems, recourse is seldom taken to direct price observations, except when a low level of imports of a given item relative to domestic use gives grounds for believing that tariffs are ineffective because of redundancy or because of strict import licensing.

COMPARATIVE REAL-INCOME STUDIES
AND LEVELS OF PROTECTION

Direct international price observations are used not only in calculating protection, but also in making comparisons of real national income in terms of purchasing-power equivalents as was done for

---

*In Pakistan, the differences between apparent tariffs and observed price differences were so wide that the correlation of the rank-orderings of 32 industries obtained by the two methods was only .35 for nominal and .36 for effective protection. (See Stephen R. Lewis, Jr., and Stephen E. Guisinger, "Measuring Protection in a Developing Country: The Case of Pakistan," Journal of Political Economy, LXXVI, 6 [November-December, 1968], 1179.)

Western Europe by Milton Gilbert and Irving B. Kravis.[8] Similar
estimates have been made in Latin America by ECLA for the years
1960 and 1962, with extrapolation for the years 1955 to 1966.[9] A more
exhaustive survey along the same lines is now underway, sponsored
by the Program of Joint Studies on Latin American Economic Integration (ECIEL) under the coordination of Joseph Grunwald and his
staff at the Brookings Institution.[10]

The question naturally arises whether the same price observations
could serve the two types of purposes. In general, the answer is that
real-income study data provide only a third-best source for estimates
of protection. The purchasing-power-parity type of inquiry is intended
primarily to provide an alternative to use of current official exchange
rates in the conversion of national accounts data into dollars, where
welfare comparisons are desired. In accordance with national accounts
definitions, only final products and services and investment goods are
included in the
of 261 consumption and 113 investment items. In measuring protection,
on the other hand, it is necessary to take account also of the raw materials
and intermediate goods which flow in international trade but are netted
out in the national product and income accounts. Purchasing-power
comparisons measure price disparity arising for any reason. Nominal
protection is concerned only with those price disparities that result
from protective measures. Furthermore, in purchasing-power-parity
studies, the comparisons are not between cif world-market prices (for
imports) and domestic factory prices (for import-substitution goods),
but between the user prices in a city in one country and those prevailing
in a city in another country. To reconcile the two pricing systems
would require making allowances for differences in trade markups, domestic indirect taxes, and transportation costs. Finally, while the
weighting problems are analogous in the two types of inquiry, these
problems are resolved differently. Whereas the purchasing-power-
parity exercise involves symmetrical binary comparisons between two
countries, in which each country's prices can be expressed in either
its own or the other's consumption or investment weights, in the measurement of protection the comparison is between the country's prices
and the full set of world prices with which it is confronted at the frontier.[1]

There is nevertheless enough overlap to justify a comparison
of the results obtained by the two approaches.

In Table 3 we have converted from implicit-exchange-rate form
to price-ratio form the purchasing-power parities calculated by ECLA
for a number of Latin American currencies as of 1962, weighted by
the Latin American pattern of expenditure.[12] The purchasing-power-
parity exchange rates calculated by ECLA for each category of national
expenditure were divided by the official or other "basic" exchange

TABLE 3

Comparison of International Price Ratios Derived from ECLA Real-Income Studies[a]
with Implicit Price Ratios Derived from Tariff Studies[b]

	(1)	(2)	(3)	(4)	(5)	(6)	(7)	(8)	(9)
		Consumption			Durable Prod.	Invent.	Trade		Official or "Basic"
Country	Year	Private	Govt.	Constr.	Goods	Changes	Balance	Total	Rate of Exchange
Argentina	1962	0.60	0.24	0.91	1.90	0.65	1.00	0.60	113. pesos/$1.00
(Chart 7, I.3)	(1962)				(2.22)				
	1964	0.72	0.28	1.05	2.38	0.77	1.00	0.70	140 ,, ,,
(Chart 2, SITC 71)	(1965)				(2.34)				
Bolivia	1962	0.65	0.24	0.67	1.42	0.72	1.00	0.60	11.9 pesos/$1.00
(Macario, Table 3)	(1959)				(1.17)				
Brazil	1962	0.66	0.52	0.89	1.78	0.71	1.00	0.69	300 cruzeiros/$1.00
(Chart 8, I.3)	(1962)				(1.84)				
	1964	0.71	0.74	1.00	1.96	0.77	1.00	0.77	903 ,, ,,
Colombia	1962	0.72	0.38	0.63	1.44	0.78	1.00	0.68	6.68 pesos/$1.00
(Chart 10, I.3)	(1962)				(1.18)				
	1964	0.84	0.48	0.67	1.47	0.94	1.00	0.79	8.58 ,, ,,
Chile	1962	0.90	0.52	0.80	1.86	0.94	1.00	0.86	1.05 escudos/$1.00
(Chart 9, I.3)	(1962)				(1.45)				
	1964	0.80	0.48	0.74	2.14	0.90	1.00	0.80	2.39 ,, ,,
Ecuador	1962	0.65	0.32	0.53	1.69	0.75	1.00	0.62	166 sucres/$1.00
(Chart 11, I.3)	(1961)				(1.67)				
Paraguay	1962	0.63	0.32	0.76	1.70	0.68	1.00	0.62	12.4 guaranis/$1.00
(Chart 13, I.3)	(1960)				(1.54)				
Peru	1962	0.60	0.26	0.62	1.31	0.65	1.00	0.56	26.8 soles/$1.00
(Chart 14, I.3)	(1959)				(1.16)				
Uruguay	1962	0.69	0.34	0.95	1.68	0.73	1.00	0.67	11.0 pesos/$1.00
(Macario, Table 3)	(1960)				(1.27)				
	1964	0.68	0.36	0.96	1.69	0.76	1.00	0.67	16.4 ,, ,,
Venezuela	1962	1.11	1.05	1.14	1.35	1.15	1.00	1.11	3.65 bolívares/$1.00
(Macario, Table 3)	(1960)				1.11				
	1964	0.90	0.85	1.04	1.18	0.93	1.00	0.91	4.50 ,, ,,
Costa Rica	1962	0.74	0.39	0.77	1.04	0.84	1.00	0.70	6.62 colones/$1.00
Dominican Republic	1962	0.98	0.48	0.84	1.36	1.19	1.00	0.90	100 pesos/$1.00
El Salvador	1962	0.77	0.45	0.65	1.18	0.91	1.00	0.72	2.50 colones/$1.00
Guatemala	1962	0.85	0.45	0.66	1.20	0.93	1.00	0.78	1.00 quetzal/$1.00
Haiti	1962	0.70	0.41	0.62	1.17	0.78	1.00	0.66	5.00 gourdes/$1.00
Honduras	1962	0.93	0.42	0.77	1.26	1.00	1.00	0.84	2.00 lempiras/$1.00
Mexico	1962	0.56	0.43	0.65	1.22	0.63	1.00	0.57	1.25 pesos/$1.00
(Chart 12, I.3)	(1962)				(1.16)				
Nicaragua	1962	0.83	0.50	0.94	1.33	0.96	1.00	0.79	7.00 córdobas/$1.00
Panama	1962	0.82	0.45	0.96	1.20	0.88	1.00	0.78	1.00 balboas/$1.00

[a]Without parentheses: Latin American quantity weights.
[b]In parentheses.

Source: Price ratios calculated from data in unpublished ECLA memorandum, "America Latina: Equivalencias del Poder Adquisitivo de la Moneda, Según Sectores Principales de Gastos, 1955-1966" (CEPAL, Sección Estudios Especiales, October 15, 1968). Implicit price ratios of tariff systems from Charts 7-14 or (Bolivia, Uruguay, Venezuela) from Santiago Macario, "Protectionism and Industrialization in Latin America," Economic Bulletin for Latin America, IX, 1, (March, 1964), Annex III.

rate (Column 9) used in the ECLA calculation as the exchange rate
applicable to the net trade balance (Column 8). The year 1962 was
selected because it corresponds best to the information in Charts
7-14 and because 1960 and 1962 were the only years for which the
ECLA study used direct price observations. (The later years, being
extrapolated by various price indices, are subject to cumulative error.
However, 1964 figures have been shown for several countries when
they were of special interest for indicating the effects of inflation
and exhange depreciation). ECLA had calculated purchasing-power-
parity exchange rates according to three different weighting schemes:
quantity weights based on a "standard" pattern of expenditure for the
Latin American region, quantity weights based on the U.S. expenditure
pattern, and the geometric mean of the first two schemes. We have
chosen the first scheme for our table because under this type of
weighting the price ratios shown for expenditure on durable producers'
goods (Column 5) should be comparable with the average levels of
nominal protection shown in implicit-price-ratio terms for capital
goods (Group 1.3) in Charts 7-14, which are based on a sample chosen
from items commonly imported into Latin America.* For Bolivia,
Uruguay, and Venezuela--countries not covered by the sample estimates
used in Charts 7-14--we have used implicit price ratios corresponding
to the arithmetic means of customs duties and other charges obtained
from a sample covering at least 85 per cent of the countries' imports
in the selected years. 13

    In view of the statistical caveats regarding the weighting and
sampling errors affecting estimates both of purchasing-power-parities
and nominal tariff levels and in view of the conceptual differences
noted above between the two approaches to measuring price disparities,
one might not expect to find much consistency at all in the results
obtained. It is therefore a pleasant surprise to find that in almost
all cases the comparison of the two types of data in Column 5 shows
fairly close numerical results (Argentina 1964-65, Brazil, Ecuador,
and Mexico) or differences in a direction generally according with
expectations based on other information. To be sure, the average
price ratio for durable producers goods indicated by the real income
study for 1962 seems rather low in comparison with the tariff-derived
estimates (1.90 vs. 2.22), when weighted at Latin American quantity
weights. On the basis of U.S. weights, however, it would have been
2.15, and it is recalled that Argentina is by far Latin America's most
industrialized country. As for the countries where the price-ratio

───────────────

    *Although both studies were done under ECLA auspices, they
were conducted as separate projects, using different market-basket
samples.

estimate based on the real-income study is about 20 per cent or more higher than the implicit price ratio derived from the identified protective measures (Bolivia, Colombia, Chile, Uruguay, and Venezuela), the differences are easily accounted for by the known existence of import prohibitions, quota restrictions, and other nontariff barriers not taken into account in the tariff averages. Thus, in Uruguay, which shows the biggest discrepancy (32 per cent), the tariff average left out of account the exchange surcharges of 40 to 150 per cent on various products and the cost of financing prior import deposits.[14] In Chile (25 per cent discrepancy), out of 27 items in the tariff sample for capital goods, nine were on the prohibited list and two were subject to licensing. In Colombia (22 per cent discrepancy), one capital-goods sample item was prohibited and 17 were under the licensing regime. Venezuela (22 per cent) also had many import license and embargo controls. That these were relaxed noticeably after the new exchange system was established in January, 1964, is reflected by the drop in the 1964 price ratio. One might wonder why Mexico, with 17 items subject to licensing out of 27 sample items, does not show a noticeable discrepancy between the two measures of nominal protection. This may have reflected the liberal licensing policy for capital goods--that is, that the tariff schedule rather than quasi-tariffs determined the price ratio in this category.

Turning attention to the price ratio for total expenditures on gross domestic product (Column 8), it is noted that in all countries (except Venezuela--a special case because of the oil industry) this was less than unity and generally within the range of 0.6 to 0.8, despite the known currency overvaluation evidenced by the protective system and/or by the balance of payments. In Venezuela, the stabilization and devaluation measures of 1964 brought the overall ratio below unity, but it was still higher than in the other countries.

In other words, in Latin American countries the "real" or welfare value of the final output of all goods and services is almost always greater than would be indicated by converting the local-currency value of goods and services at official exchange rates, and this is especially true where Latin American weights are used. Poor countries are not as poor as they look because they get more for a dollar's worth of local currency than a dollar will buy in the United States. For this to be true, even when nominal protection may be more than doubling the relative prices of imports and import-substitutables, *

---

*It is recalled that capital goods, the only "tradable" category shown in Table 3, have the lowest levels of protection in most South American countries.

means that the relative prices of nontraded goods and services
(including government services) that people consume must be very
much lower than in the United States, and that a large part of the
gross domestic product is spent on nontradables.

Edmar Bacha and Lance Taylor[15] used price information from
the ECLA real-income study to calculate an indicative average level
of nominal protection in Chile in 1962. They made no allowance for
protection on input products. Among other assumptions, they assumed
"that the ratio between international prices and Chilean prices cif-
Santiago is adequately approximated by the ratio between minimum
user's prices in the LAFTA area and user's prices in Chile." For
example, the Chilean prices for the meat, dairy, cereals, fats and
oils, alcoholic beverages, electrical appliances, and office machinery
components of the Latin American market basket were compared with
corresponding prices in Argentina. Brazilian prices were used as
the basis for comparison for household utensils, toilet articles, phar-
maceuticals, books, and toys. Ecuador was the reference country for
fish, fruit, clothing, and footwear; Colombian prices were used for
textiles. To the extent that the comparison country itself had some
positive nominal protection on the products in question, this method
would appear to underestimate the level of protection.

David Felix[16] has used the price ratios obtained from the ECLA
real-income study to measure the bias of Argentine import substitution
in favor of "dynamic" manufacturing industries, as compared with
"vegetative" manufacturing industries. Although this is not made
very explicit in his text, Felix was actually using the price ratios to
measure levels of protection.

The conclusion reached from this digression is that a number
of insights could be obtained by more systematically linking the study
of protection (viewed as a system of relative prices) with the parallel
research into interspatial price relationships that is being carried
out in connection with real-income comparisons. Moreover, when it
is impractical to obtain direct price observations suitable for estimation of nominal protection, disaggregated data on relative prices
derived from real-income studies may provide a useful "third-best"
substitute. However, this method furnishes data only for those final-
demand products covered by expenditure on gross domestic product
(consumption and investment goods, but not raw materials or intermediate inputs).

HOW "ACCURATE" ARE STATISTICAL
ESTIMATES OF EFFECTIVE PROTECTION?

The preceding pages have stressed the complexities of

classification, weighting, sampling, etc., with which any attempts to quantify and aggregate levels of protection must cope. Yet these are relatively straightforward statistical problems, similar to those arising in construction of other types of price-index numbers. If it were not for the fact that tariffs touch particularly sensitive economic and political interests, domestically and abroad, some internationally acceptable arrangements for regular collection, processing, and publication of data on nominal protection would doubtless exist already.

Calculation of effective protection is an entirely different matter. Estimates of nominal tariff rates on outputs and inputs, which are themselves subject to errors of observation and aggregation, are run through a mathematical transformation that amplifies these errors and combines them with additional errors of observation and aggregation inherent in input-output tables.[17] It has been seen that differences of methodology with respect to treatment of nontraded inputs, adjustment for currency overvaluation, deflation of values in domestic input-output tables to world prices, etc., can radically change the numerical results. The figures are also sensitive to failure of the arbitrary assumptions underlying the input-output technique to be fulfilled in practice. Production functions do differ internationally and change over time; existence of decreasing cost industries and external economics cannot realistically be assumed away. Definitions of sectors for input-output purposes may be inappropriate for evaluating protection. A number of fundamental criticisms of the concept of effective protection, at least in the Barber-Johnson-Corden-Balassa formulation, have been made by W.P. Travis[18] and Roy J. Ruffin,[19] although most of these appear to have been satisfactorily answered.[20] Finally, because effective rates are usually higher than the more familiar nominal tariff rates, there has been some abuse of the effective-tariff approach for propagandistic purposes, especially in the UNCTAD forum. In this connection it should be noted that international comparison of the average height of effective tariffs is meaningless. The effective-tariff concept should be used only to analyze and compare patterns of protection.[21]

Despite these criticisms, it can be agreed that ranking industries in an ascending scale of levels of effective protection tells us something about comparative advantage and, in conjunction with other techniques (programming and "shadow" prices), provides objective criteria helpful for selection of viable investment projects. More important, the effective-protection approach puts tariff-making and tariff reform on a more scientific foundation. While many countries will continue to be protectionist-oriented, more often than not to their own disadvantage, increased awareness of the fact that a tariff system taxes inputs as well as raising output prices will at least eliminate some of the structural incoherence--such as reverse escalation--that has characterized Latin American tariff structures in the past.

For most purposes, the relative ranking of industries and processes in terms of effective protection is more important than precision of estimation in any absolute sense. Since estimates of effective protection can be no better, and may be much worse, than the nominal-protection data on which they are based, and since inspection of the profile of nominal protection tells much about what effective protection is likely to be, first priority should be given to improving the available estimates according to the less sophisticated concept.

NOTES

1. League of Nations, Tariff Level Indices, 1927 (Geneva, 1927).

2. Bela Balassa and Associates, The Structure of Protection in Developing Countries (Baltimore: Johns Hopkins Press, 1971). Chapter 1.

3. UNCTAD Research Memorandum No. 13/4 of December 18, 1967, ''Methodological and Technical Notes on UNCTAD Tariff Profiles.'' (Unpublished.)

4. References to documentation (mainly classified '' restricted'') on the sample studies are listed in Asociación Latinoamericana de Libre Comercio (ALALC), Grupo de estudio sobre arancel externo común, Relación Sucinta de las Labores Realizadas en la Segunda Etapa de la Tercera Reunión (CEP/GE.AEC/Informe 4, 23 de setiembre de 1968).

5. Hugo Opazo, '' La armonización de los sistemas aduaneros de los paises de la ALALC,'' in Instituto para la Integración de América Latina (INTAL), Hacia una Tarifa Externa Común en América Latina (Buenos Aires: INTAL, 1969), p. 121.

6. Cf. Stephen R. Lewis, Jr., '' Effects of Trade Policy on Domestic Relative Prices: Pakistan, 1951-1964,'' American Economic Review, LVIII, 2 (March, 1968), Appendix.

7. Balassa and Associates, op. cit., Chapter 1.

8. Milton Gilbert and Irving B. Kravis, An International Comparison of National Products and the Purchasing Power of Currencies (Paris: Organization for Economic Cooperation and Development, 1954).

9. Economic Commission for Latin America, '' The Measurement of Latin American Real Incomes in U.S. Dollars,'' Economic Bulletin for Latin America, XII, 2,107-42; Economic Commission for Latin America, A Measurement of Price Levels and the Purchasing Powers of Currencies in Latin America, 1960-62 (ECLA document E/CN.12/653, March 31, 1963) Stanley N. Braithwaite, ''Real Income Levels in Latin America,'' The Review of Income and Wealth, 14, 2 (June, 1968).

10. '' International Price and Real-Income Comparisons,'' coordinated by Jorge Salazar of the Brookings Institution. A related Brookings/ECIEL project, ''Study on Industrial Efficiency,'' coordinated by Peter B. Knight, will also develop comparative price information with respect to inputs and outputs of seven industries in eleven Latin American Countries.

11. The conceptual differences between the purposes implicit exchange rates and purchasing-power-parity exchange rates a la Gilbert-Kravis have been discussed by Stephen R. Lewis, Jr., in Implicit Exchange Rates, Relative Prices, and Efficiency of Industrial Growth in Pakistan (Williamstown, Mass.: Center for Development Economics, Williams College, 1966), pp. vi-2.

12. ''América Latina: Equivalencias del Poder Adquisitivo de la Moneda, Según Sectores Principales de Gastos, 1955-1966'' (unpublished memorandum, CEPAL, Sección Estudios Especiales, October 15, 1968.

13. Santiago Macario, '' Protectionism and Industrialization in Latin America, Economic Bulletin for Latin America, IX, 1 (March, 1964), 70.

14. Ibid., 68.

15. Edmar Bacha and Lance Taylor, Foreign Exchange Shadow Prices in Chile: Conflicting Theories and Comparative Evaluations (Santiago: Oficina de Planificación Nacional, October, 1969), pp. 40 ff.

16. David Felix, '' Import Substitution, '' in Gustav V. Papanek, ed., Development Policy: Theory and Practice (Cambridge, Mass.: Harvard University Press, 1968), p. 85.

17. See J. Clark Leith, '' The Specification of Nominal Tariff Rates in Effective Protection Estimates,'' AID/Wisconsin Research Project on Economic Interdependence in Southeast Asia, No. 12 (October, 1966), pp. 4-9.

18. W. P. Travis, The Effective Rate of Protection and the Question of Labor Protection in the United States, Journal of Political Economy (May-June, 1968), pp. 443-45.

19. Roy J. Ruffin, Tariffs, Intermediate Goods, and Domestic Protection, American Economic Review, LIX, 3 (June, 1969), 261-69.

20. The rebuttal of Travis is contained in Bela Balassa, Stephen E. Guisinger, and Daniel M. Schydlowsky, The Effective Rates of Protection and the Question of Labor Protection in the United States: A Comment, Journal of Political Economy, LXXVIII, 5 (September-October, 1970), 1150-62; Balassa's reply to Ruffin is in Tariffs, Intermediate Goods, and Domestic Protection: Comment, American Economic Review, LX, 5 (December, 1970), 959-69.

21. Cf. James E. Anderson, General Equilibrium and the Effective Rate of Protection, Journal of Political Economy, LXXVIII, 4, Part 1 (July-August, 1970, 723.

4

INTERNATIONAL
AND INTERTEMPORAL
COMPARISONS OF
PROTECTIVE STRUCTURES
OF LAFTA COUNTRIES

The preceding chapters have been devoted to establishing a conceptual framework for measurement and analysis of the heterogeneous protective structures of Latin America, emphasizing the influence of protection in determining relationships between domestic and international prices. Subsequent chapters will apply this approach to a survey of selected commercial-policy issues that are of particular importance in the context of the efforts toward Latin American integration. At this point, it may be useful to give an overall conspectus of the protective regimes of a number of Latin American countries, specifically those belonging to the Latin American Free Trade Association. In lieu of a detailed country-by-country description, which would be beyond the scope of this study, an attempt is made to summarize, statistically, the countries' nominal tariffs as of the beginning and end of the 1960's, showing how they might be ranked according to two indicators of protectionism: the average height and the degree of dispersion of nominal tariff levels.

The term "indicators of protectionism" is used, for want of a less-connotative expression, to show that we are seeking to identify and quantify policy parameters (or variables) that represent numerically the characteristic objective features of measures taken under an import-substitution strategy. These features (which will be discussed at some length in Chapter 6) usually include discouragement of exports, discrimination against agriculture and other primary production, relatively low protection on investment goods; unusually steep escalation of rates as among categories; and minute differentiation of rates on closely related products.

The common characteristic is dispersion of nominal rates of protection (and a fortiori of effective protection). It has been pointed out that an undifferentiated high tariff matched by a uniform export

subsidy would be indistinguishable from free trade at a devalued exchange rate. However, since tariffs are seldom symmetrically matched
by subsidies on exports, and it is common for exports to be only mod-
erately subsidized or even subject to negative protection in the form
of export taxes, the average height of the import tariff can be taken
as a rough measure of the disparity between the level of protection
on imports and that on exports, which disparity is in itself an important element of dispersion of the protective system. The other characteristics of import-substitution policies, besides the discrimination
against exporting, are reflected in the dispersion of the import-tariff
levels among different kinds of imports. Thus, although it is convenient to use two sets of indicators, distinguishing between the treatment of exports and that of imports, both refer to dispersion of rates
applicable to particular products (exports or imports) as compared
with a hypothetical uniform-exchange-rate level with zero tariffs.
The two measures could be combined multiplicatively in various ways
if a single index of protectionism were desired.

Table 4 shows unweighted import "tariff" averages for a number of Latin American countries as of about 1962 (based on the ECLA
sample data underlying Charts 7-14) and more or less comparable
averages as of about 1968 (based on data from the LAFTA "experimental sample" described in Chapter 3). It must be stressed that
the only respects in which the two sample market baskets are similar
is that they are both unweighted, disaggregated at the item level, and
representative of categories covering most import trade (although it
has been seen that the LAFTA sample has serious lacunae). The
fact that they are both unweighted at least provides assurance that
the arithmetic means of the data are not biased downwards by own-
trade weighting--the worst vice of most attempts to average tariffs.
However, since unweighted averages have their own intrinsic weights,
it is of interest to see to what extent the results are sensitive to the
level of aggregation. For this reason there are shown not only item-
level averages but also (in parentheses) the averages of the group
and subgroup classifications used in the LAFTA sample. It is interesting to note that the two methods of averaging heights of tariffs
give very close results in most, but not all, cases.

The fact that both samples cover a wide range of categories of
traded goods and that they are both disaggregated at the item level
suggests that the sample standard deviations might provide estimators
of relative variability that would be sufficiently comparable to have
informational interest. However, for reasons discussed in Chapter
1, it was considered more useful to show, in Table 5, the standard
deviations relative to implicit price ratios rather than in terms of
tariff rates, because normalizing the data in relative price units
avoids distortion of proportionality.

TABLE 4

Estimates of Average Height of Tariffs,
Including Certain Other Charges and Exchange Premia
(in percentage points)

Circa 1962		Circa 1968		
ECLA sample (125 items, unweighted)		LAFTA sample (299 items, unweighted)		(31 groups or subgroups)
Brazil (X)	170	Chile	177	(166)
		Uruguay (X)	160	(184)
Argentina (X)	137			
Chile	134			
Colombia (Q)	106			
		Paraguay (X)	85	(83)
		Ecuador (X)	76	(81)
		Argentina	76	(74)
		AVERAGE	75	(78)
Paraguay (X)	70	Peru	68	(63)
Mexico (Q)	62			
Ecuador	61			
		Mexico (Q)	48	(50)
		Colombia (Q)	44	(49)
		Brazil	42	(43)
Peru	35	Venezuela (Q)	35	(45)
		Bolivia		(26)

(X) = Exchange surcharge included in "tariff"
(Q) = In addition to "tariffs", country used quantitative restrictions on imports (effect not shown)

Sources: Circa 1962 -- Charts 6 to 14
          Circa 1968 -- Calculated from LAFTA experimental sample (fascículo 1)

65

TABLE 5

Estimates of Relative Variability of Implicit Price Ratios
Corresponding to Tariffs, Other Charges, and Exchange Premia
(in coefficients of variation)

Circa 1962		Circa 1968	
ECLA sample (125 items, unweighted)		LAFTA sample (299 items, unweighted)	(31 groups or subgroups)
Chile	0.97	Chile 1.00	(0.37)
Colombia (Q)	0.86		
Mexico (Q)	0.58		
Brazil (X)	0.50		
Argentina (X)	0.44		
Peru	0.44	Venezuela (Q) 0.41	(0.30)
		Ecuador (X) 0.39	(0.20)
		Peru 0.39	(0.19)
Ecuador	0.37		
		Uruguay (X) 0.36	(0.24)
Paraguay	0.35	Bolivia 0.35	(0.13)
		Mexico (Q) 0.32	(0.19)
		AVERAGE 0.26	(0.16)
		Colombia (Q) 0.25	(0.26)
		Argentina 0.21	(0.17)
		Brazil 0.19	(0.17)
		Paraguay (X) 0.17	(0.12)

(X) = Exchange surcharge included in "tariff"
(Q) = In addition to "tariffs," country used quantitative restrictions on imports (effect not shown)

Sources: Circa 1962--Charts 6 to 14
Circa 1968--Calculated from LAFTA experimental sample (fascículo 1)

66

In order to test whether there is any approximate accuracy in the numerical results shown in Tables 4 and 5, they have been checked against other available information. This was possible for Argentina and Brazil, for which unweighted sample data at the item level happened to be available for about the same periods. As can be seen from Table 6, there is remarkable consistency both with respect to the tariff averages and with respect to coefficients of variation.

It is of greater substantive interest, however, to see whether the indicators tell a story that makes sense in the light of the known history of the respective tariff systems between 1962 and 1968.

The principal changes shown on the two charts are those of Brazil and Argentina, both of which countries undertook, in 1967, major reforms of their tariff systems. The scope of the Argentine reform has already been illustrated in Chapter 1.

In view of the frequent devaluations and changes in the Brazilian multiple-rate regimes over the last decade and a half, the most appropriate way of visualizing the evolution of that country's protective structure is perhaps by means of a chart of implicit exchange rates for various categories of products. Chart 16, which is on a logarithmic scale, plots the vagaries of the profile of protection for a number of years. Compared to the peaks and valleys shown for previous years, the 1967 profile is relatively flat.

The indicated improvement shown for Colombia's tariff structure (reduction of average tariff and of the dispersion indicator) may have reflected mainly the erosion of specific tariffs accompanying the approximate doubling of the peso-dollar exchange rate between 1962 and 1968. The history of Colombian commercial and exchange policy during the intervening period was too confused and confusing to recapitulate here, but it is questionable whether the tariff reform of 1965, which put all duties on an ad valorem basis, significantly reduced the level and dispersion of protection. The estimates based on the LAFTA sample would appear to exaggerate any net improvement, in part because of the limitations on the product coverage of the sample. As already noted, the automotive sector is not covered at all, yet the range in tariffs on automotive vehicles is reportedly to be currently from 2 to 450 per cent.[1] In any case, quantitative restrictions rather than tariffs have been the major influence on allocation of imports, and, as noted on Tables 4 and 5, no estimates for the effect of such quasi-tariffs have been included in our figures. In view of the frequent criticisms of the high degree of dispersion in the Colombian protective structure, the classification of Colombia at the lower end of the ranking in Table 5 is perhaps misleading.[2]

TABLE 6

Cross-check of Estimated Indicators of "Protectionism"
Shown in Tables 4 and 5

		average "tariffs" $\bar{t}$	coefficients of variation $\dfrac{s}{ipr}$
Argentina			
Prereform			
1962	ECLA sample (cf. Chart 7)		
	Table 6	137	
	Table 8		0.44
1965	UNCTAD sample (cf. Chart 2)	157	0.42
Postreform			
1968	LAFTA sample (cf. Chart 16)		
	Table 6	76	
	Table 7		0.21
1967	UNCTAD sample (cf. Chart 3)	69	0.23
Brazil			
Prereform			
1962	ECLA sample (cf. Chart 8)		
	Table 6	170	
	Table 7		0.50
1964	Clark sample[a](cf. Chart 16)	138	0.47
(1962)	(Clark--extrapolated back[b])	(162)	
Postreform			
1968	LAFTA sample		
	Table 6	42	
	Table 7		0.19
1967	Clark sample[c]	39	n.a.

[a] Paul G. Clark and Richard Weisskoff, "Import Demands and Import Policies in Brazil" (February, 1967), Table B-2B (unweighted average, tariff and exchange protection).

[b] Ibid., Table B.4A (extrapolated by change in weighted average).

[c] Paul G. Clark, "Brazilian Import Liberalization" (September, 1967), Table 1a (unweighted averages, tariff & exchange protection, extrapolated by change in weighted averages, Table 1b).

CHART 16

Brazil: Nominal Protection Profiles
of "Implicit Exchange Rates"*
by Use Classes, 1953-67

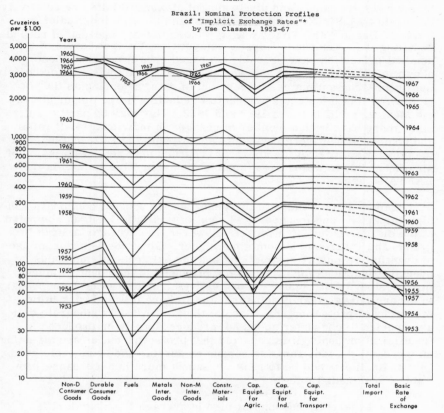

*Implicit exchange rates are (1+E)r, where E is the average tariff rate plus exchange premium
for a use class, and r is the basic exchange rate.

Sources: Paul G. Clark and Richard Weisskoff, "Import Demands and Import Policies in Brazil,"
(February, 1967); Paul G. Clark, "Brazilian Import Liberalization" (September, 1967).

69

Mexico and Venezuela are the two other major Latin American countries where the failure of the indicators to take account of the price effects of quantitative restrictions makes the numerical results difficult to interpret, since goods representing about 65 percent by value of Mexico's total import trade are subject to import licenses.[3] In any case, the height and dispersion of Mexican tariffs are relatively moderate by Latin American standards, and the detailed studies by Gerardo Bueno [4] and Timothy King [5] indicate that, because of redundancy resulting from vigorous domestic competition, the true levels of nominal protection have probably averaged even lower than those shown in Table 4, which are based on the tariff samples. Unfortunately, the Bueno-King estimates are very out of date, referring as they do to 1960. Table 5 indicates substantial reduction in the dispersion of the Mexican tariff between 1962 and 1968. This may be partly real, since there have been a number of changes in individual tariff rates and nomenclatures were revised to accord with the BTN in 1965. On the other hand, part of the apparent progress may reflect omission of significant import categories (notably the automotive sector) in the LAFTA sample.

Tables 4 and 5 indicate for Venezuela an unusual combination of high variability and low average height of tariffs in 1968, as computed at the disaggregated (item) level. However, the average tariff of the groups and subgroups is somewhat higher. Given the Venezuelan use of quantitative import restrictions and the existence of numerous special exemptions for products not produced in the country, much further study of that country's protective structure would be necessary in order to draw clear conclusions as to where it would rank in the hierarchy of protectionism. Despite the fact that only moderate duties are applied to consumer goods not produced locally or produced in insufficient amounts, it is reported that protective duties are affecting an increasingly wide range of consumer durable and nondurable goods. Our inclination would be to rank Venezuela more in accordance with Table 5 than with Table 6.

The apparently substantial rise in average Peruvian tariffs between 1960 and 1968 probably gives a reasonably true picture, in view of the fact that a new tariff schedule with generally much higher rates was introduced in June, 1967, and this tends to be confirmed by cursory spot-checks of a number of individual items for which the ECLA and LAFTA sample data overlap.

The unusual lack of variability shown for the Paraguayan protective structure in 1968 reflects the fact that almost one-third of the total ''tariff'' is accounted for by a uniform 32 per cent foreign-exchange surcharge applied to most non-LAFTA imports.

Uruguay is another case where application of exchange surcharges tends to reduce somewhat the variability of the total "tariff," even though there are six different basic rates of surcharge ranging from 30 to 300 per cent of cif value. In any case, the Uruguayan protective structure is about tied with that of Chile insofar as height of "tariff" is concerned, and attention has already been called to the fact that its commercial-cum-exchange policy regime is about as confusing as can be imagined.

Judged by either the height or dispersion of protective rates, Chile probably has the most distorted price system (as judged by the criterion of the world market relationships) to be found in Latin America, and the situation has undoubtedly deteriorated during the 1960's. As of late 1969, it seemed that steps were being taken to prepare for a reform, reflecting the belated awareness of the bureaucracy that the country's notorious structural inefficiencies were not unrelated to the systematically perverse incentives built into the foreign-trade regime, and that Chile could hardly play the leading role in the Andean Group to which it aspired without a thorough housecleaning at home. Since that time, new political groups have come to power. It is premature to judge the Allende Government's program--if any-- in this area of economic policy, but the composition of the new team does not suggest that changes will be in the direction of reliance on price and market mechanisms.

NOTES

1. Richard R. Nelson, Robert L. Slighton, and Paul Schultz, Colombian Development Policy (unpublished Rand Corporation study, December, 1969), p. 64.

2. John B. Sheahan, "Imports, Investment, and Growth," and Harold B. Dunkerley, "Exchange Rate Systems in Conditions of Continuing Inflation--Lessons from Colombian Experience," in Gustav V. Papanek, Development Policy: Theory and Practice (Cambridge, Mass.: Harvard University Press, 1968), pp. 93-174; John Sheahan and Sara Clark, The Response of Colombian Exports to Variations in Effective Exchange Rates, Research Memorandum No. 11 (Williamstown, Mass.: Center for Development Economics, Williams College, June, 1967); and Antonio Urdinola and Richard Mallon, Policies to Promote Colombian Exports of Manufactures (AID/Harvard project ERP I I I-117, Economic Development Report No. 75, preliminary draft, date unknown).

3. U.S. Department of Commerce, Foreign Trade Regulations of Mexico (Bureau of International Commerce, OBR 66-62, October, 1966).

4. Gerardo Bueno, ''The Structure of Protection in Mexico,'' in Balassa and Associates, The Structure of Protection in Some Developing Countries (Baltimore: Johns Hopkins Press, 1971), Chapter 8.

5. Timothy King, forthcoming book in the OECD Development Center Series. (Section on protective structure based mainly on Bueno.)

RELATIONSHIP BETWEEN COMPARATIVE ADVANTAGE AND PROFILES OF PROTECTION

According to classical static comparative cost theory, [1] welfare is usually maximized when countries specialize in production of those products for which they have a comparative advantage. This is determined by the relative opportunity costs of obtaining the same goods through foreign trade. "Under the assumptions of full employment and perfect competition, the opportunity cost of a commodity, which is the value of the factors used to produce it in their best alternative employment, is equal to its market value. Market prices of factors and commodities can therefore be used to determine comparative advantage under competitive conditions." [2] Since levels of nominal protection are defined in terms of ratios between domestic and world-market prices, it would appear that comparing the levels of nominal protection on different categories of goods should directly indicate a country's comparative cost structure. Moreover, when the tariff is fully utilized, and in the absence of nonprice protection (i.e., when the tariff faithfully reflects the price disparities among tradable goods), it might seem that the profile of protection implied by the tariff and tariff-like measures would be a sufficient indicator of comparative advantage. For a number of reasons, however, such an inference would be misleading as a guide to efficient resource allocation.

In the first place, this concept of comparative advantage is purely static and does not take into account the fact that comparative advantage can, does, and should change over time. Indeed, one of the most respectable arguments for protection--the infant-industry argument--is based on the fact that there is a learning process in economic development and that, after a certain threshold of sheltered production is passed, internal economies of scale and various types of external economies may reduce the comparative cost of a given industry.

73

Furthermore, there are a number of reasons why market prices may
not reflect the true opportunity cost of factors. One of these is that,
due to factor-price distortions that are believed to be particularly prevalent in underdeveloped countries, there is likely to be a substantial
divergence between private cost and social cost. Monopoly and other
market-structure rigidities (many of which are created or preserved
by protection itself), together with existence of decreasing-cost industries, also tend to break the nexus between comparative costs and
observed market prices. Because the assumptions of the classical
model with respect to perfect competition, full employment, and initial
equilibrium fail to be fulfilled in real-life situations, the doctrine of
comparative advantage has come to be considerably watered down.
The weaker Heckscher-Ohlin version[3] merely states that a country
benefits from specializing in the production of those goods that use
more of its relatively abundant factors of production. This doctrine,
which suggests that less-developed countries will have a comparative
advantage in labor-intensive and resource-intensive production, has
also been challenged on a number of grounds because it in turn rests
on restrictive assumptions, notably with respect to international comparability of factors of production and of production functions.[4] Recent
empirical work has, however, tended to confirm the main part of the
Heckscher-Ohlin theory.[5]

Another difficulty of using classical comparative advantage as a
guide to allocational efficiency lies in the assumption that the exchange
rates of the countries under consideration are at their equilibrium
levels and that such equilibria in the exchange market will be maintained
over time. As a practical matter, exchange rates in most countries
are pegged and considerable balance-of-payments pressure may develop
before chronic overvaluation is corrected. To be sure, exchange rates
are more mobile in Latin America than elsewhere, and several countries
(notably Brazil and Chile) are now making frequent adjustments more
or less in line with the rate of domestic inflation. As a practical matter,
however, absolute advantage, indicated by direct disparities between
domestic and foreign prices at the existing exchange rate, is of more
immediate importance to policy-makers than is the comparative
advantage shown by the ratios among the price ratios for the array of
products.

This point can be illustrated by a model devised by Daniel M.
Schydlowsky for analysis of the process of integration in Latin America.[6]
Using a linear-programming analytical framework, Schydlowsky
describes a dynamic process of trade liberalization in which, starting
from a given pattern of absolute advantage at given exchange rates,
the negotiation of concessions generates new net flows of trade within
the integration area and with third countries. These in turn determine
new exchange-rate relationships and a new situation of absolute advantage among the countries. This process of trade liberalization and
successive cross-rate adjustments is reiterated as each country

continues to follow an optimal bargaining strategy of demanding
and offering concessions on all the products in which it has an absolute
advantage. If carried on long enough, the process converges on an
equilbrium solution corresponding to that which would have been indicated by comparative advantage, the latter being defined in a dynamic
long-run sense, i.e., taking account of economies of scale, the learning process, etc. The lesson of this exercise is that the principle of
comparative advantage only works out as a guide to policy over the long
run and if there is a balance-of-payments adjustment mechanism. In
the short run, the negotiability of trade liberalization concessions in
an integration grouping is likely to be limited by the pattern of absolute
advantage and by the availability of finance to cover deficits.

Turning to the question whether the profile of protection can be
used to provide a scale of comparative advantage, it must be reempha-
sized that much depends on how one measures protection. In the first
place, when talking about comparative advantage or resource allocation,
we are talking about those relative prices that are derived from actual
international price disparities and which are not necessarily the same
as those implied by the tariff schedule. Secondly, since we are concerned with costs of production, our interest is in the productive process and not simply in the final outputs. This means that adjustment
must be made, not only for domestic indirect taxes, and the like, but
also for the effects of the nominal protection on material inputs. In
other words, it is the profile of effective protection that is relevant,
not just the profile of nominal protection, and even the profile of effective protection claims only to give a ranking by comparative advantage
under certain restrictive assumptions.* Moreover, the profiles of
a country's nominal and effective protection on individual products and
activities may vary erratically over time in accordance with vagaries
of governmental decision-making. The underlying scale of comparative
advantage of the economy, on the other hand, is unlikely to fluctuate
much in the short run. Finally, effective protection estimates are
usually available only for broad aggregates of activities, including some
that enjoy a comparative advantage and others that do not. All that one
can say is that highly differentiated profiles of effective protection
establish a strong presumption "that some industries, or parts of
industries or plants, in these countries either should never have been
set up at all, because there was no hope of their ever yielding a good
social return to the country; or policies have been such that they were
set up in the wrong way, or have been such as to prevent their achieving

---

*The principal assumptions are that production functions are of
the Cobb-Douglas form, that there is perfect competition, that there is
marginal-cost pricing, and that there is no substitution between primary
factors and material inputs.

adequate efficiency. [7] Still, this is worth knowing, and that existence
of a high average level of effective protection for a sector, or of a non-
spurious case of negative value added in a sector, is good prima facie
evidence of where to look for trouble.

COSTS OF PROTECTION

What is the cost imposed on an economy by serious misallo-
cation of resources through extreme protectionism of the South American type? Depending on the method of evaluation and on the structural
parameters of the national economy involved, the answer can vary
over a wide range. According to Harry Johnson's model, which uses
static welfare analysis, imposition of tariffs involves two kinds of
losses of welfare: first, a loss of utility on the production side from
the reduction of real output below the level possible under free trade
and second, a loss of consumption utility from nonoptimal expenditure
of the reduced real income. Johnson concluded that

> both the total gains from international trade and the cost
> of protection are likely to be relatively small in the large
> industrial countries, owing to their relatively flexible eco-
> nomic structures, probably high elasticity of substitution
> among the goods on which consumption is concentrated,
> and relatively low natural dependence on trade; while
> they are likely to be appreciably larger, relative to
> maximum potential national income, in the smaller and
> less developed countries, whose economies tend to show
> the opposite characteristics. [8]

Applying Johnson's formula to hypothetical 100 per cent import tariff
(not unusual in Latin America) and to the intermediate part of the
range of possible structural parameters, the total loss of utility due
to protection might be of the order of about 12.5 per cent of national
income, of which about 8 percentage points might be accounted for by
production loss and about 4 or 5 per cent accounted for by consumption
loss. The maximum total welfare loss for which Johnson provided in
his model would be twice that much (25 per cent), in an extreme case
of absolute autarchy. While this order of magnitude would explain
only part of the difference of income in developing countries below
levels prevailing in industrial countries, Johnson pointed out that such
a loss of real income from protection nevertheless looms very large
when one considers the cost--in terms of incremental investment or
sacrificed growth-- that would be involved in replacing this loss by a
corresponding increase in income.

In 1958, Arnold Harberger estimated that the welfare loss due to protection in a country like Chile would not exceed 2.5 per cent of national income.[9] Bela Balassa challenged several of Harberger's assumptions, pointing out that average Chilean nominal protection may have been as much as three times as high as the estimate on which Harberger's conclusion was predicated. Using revised estimates of nominal protection, Balassa concluded that the Welfare cost would be somewhere between 10.5 and 21 per cent of Chilean national income, (a range that happens to be consistent with that suggested by Johnson's method). Balassa went on to point out that the calculation should have been based on the effective protection concept.[10]

Because of problems of aggregation and difficulties of measuring the elasticities and other parameters of the models, any such quantitative estimates of welfare loss attributable to protection at the microeconomic level should be viewed with suspicion. However, study of individual industries confirms the general conclusion that developing countries in general, and South American countries in particular, have sacrificed much potential real income to exaggerated protection.[11]

SPECIALIZATION BY INDUSTRIES AND SPECIALIZATION WITHIN INDUSTRIES

Because industrial and trade statistics, in order to be manageable, are usually grouped in more or less broad categories, it is customary to interpret comparative advantage in terms of the same levels of aggregation. This implies that all the products or activities of the category use the same inputs and combinations of factors of production, an assumption that may be very far from the truth. The problem is further complicated by the fact that industrial statistics may be collected either according to type of output or by establishment. A given establishment may, of course, produce a mix of entirely different commodities, involving different production functions.

Moreover, it has been seen that the variation of a protective structure within categories is frequently wider than that between categories. This may reflect shortcomings in the system of statistical classification, whereby economically dissimilar products or activities have been grouped under the same aggregative heading. On the other hand, it may also reflect inconsistency in the tariff-setting process. Thus, under the Brazilian "law of similars," which has its counterpart in the import-substitution policies of a number of Latin American countries, the fact that domestic production of a certain product has been embarked upon automatically carries with it a privileged level of protection for that product. At the same time, another product having many of the same economic characteristics, and which could as well have been produced locally, will be relatively unprotected. Frequently,

an identical product will be under different import regimes, depending
on whether the end user is a governmental or other specially favored
enterprise. For these reasons, such statements as "Country A has
a comparative advantage in machine tools relative to agricultural
equipment" may be very misleading.

The response of trade flows to economic integration among
industrial countries has recently forced economists to pay relatively
more attention to intraindustry specialization and to question general-
izations about comparative advantage at the industry-by-industry level.
Using the concept of revealed comparative advantage, Balassa has
pointed out that in the European Common Market the clearest cases
of interindustry specialization where the commodities or industries
in question are at the two ends of the comparative scale revealed by
actual trade flows have involved standardized products, many of which
are in the relatively homogeneous semimanufactured categories.[12]
Balassa noted, on the basis of various statistical tests, that most of
the increase in trade within the EEC involved a two-way trade within
categories: that is, specialization has been predominantly of the
intraindustry rather than the interindustry type. The welfare gains
from this increasingly diversified trade pattern would appear to come
more from economies of scale and from greater consumer choice
than from economies of resource allocation. It was observed, moreover, that intraindustry specialization tended to cushion the short-run
adverse impact of trade liberalization, at least among industrialized
countries; indeed, bankruptcies had actually declined since formation
of the EEC, and there was little evidence of frictional unemployment.

Herbert G. Grubel[13] has also concerned himself with intraindustry specialization. While agreeing with much of Balassa's analysis,
he has chosen to place more emphasis on the hypothesis that this type
of market interpenetration reflects the market imperfection characteristic of products highly differentiated by quality, style, or design as
discussed in the theories of Chamberlin and Joan Robinson. This
emphasis on monopolistic competition recalls the three-way classification used by Roy F. Harrod[14] in explaining the difference in compar-
ative-price-level behavior of A goods (relatively homogeneous products
having well-defined international prices), B goods (quasi-international
goods characterized by monopolistic competition, price-stickiness,
and decreasing costs), and C goods (services and nontradable goods
for which there is no world price level--the kind of goods and services
which determine the wide international divergence of prices shown in
real-income studies). Harrod pointed out that, although prices of B
goods tend toward a common level, they have to overcome greater
friction than in the case of A goods. (They also are frequently subject
to relatively high protection.) In understanding how comparative costs
are transmitted into relative prices motivating private traders, it is

useful to take account of the different behavior of A, B, and C goods. International differences in factor endowment and efficiency in making A and B commodities explain the differences in relative price levels that are evidenced mainly in C goods but also, to some extent, in B goods.

It will be brought out in Chapter 8 that the complementarity agreements of the Latin American Free Trade Association are designed to encourage intraindustry specialization, rather than the type of international division of labor that is associated with the principle of comparative advantage.

PROJECT EVALUATION TECHNIQUES

Measurement of comparative advantage is not just an academic exercise. One practical application is for purposes of evaluation of the total performance of an economy with respect to welfare, utilization of foreign aid, and export promotion, and especially in connection with major reforms of the tariff and foreign-exchange systems. At the microeconomic level, considerations of comparative advantage find practical application in the selection of specific industrial projects for public or private investment.

Most project selection procedures fall under the general heading of cost-benefit analysis, a discipline that is deceptively simple in concept but which may involve extremely sophisticated planning techniques: linear programming, sensitivity analysis, input-output analysis, calculation of discounted cash flow, internal rates of return on investment, comparison of private vs. social costs (or benefits), comparison of direct vs. total costs, etc.[15]

For present purposes, we are interested mainly in the part of cost-benefit analysis that ranks investment projects for comparative advantage (taken in the dynamic sense) and usually in terms of some sort of shadow or accounting price of foreign advantage.

Strictly speaking, shadow prices have a special technical meaning. They are produced in the dual solution of a linear or nonlinear programming exercise.[16] Shadow prices can be calculated for individual products, factors of production, foreign exchange, or any other resource the scarcity of which affects the choice of an optimal (or suboptimal) course of action from among the feasible alternatives bounded by the constraints imposed in the programming problem. More broadly and less rigorously, the term is used rather interchangeably with Jan Tinbergen's notion of accounting prices: "those that would prevail if (1) the investment pattern under discussion were actually carried out, and (2) equilibrium existed on the . . . labor, capital, and foreign exchange markets'' and which reflect the opportunity costs implied by a given resource allocation. [17]

As applied to the choice of export-promoting or import-substituting investment projects, the shadow or accounting price of foreign exchange is intended to reflect the true or intrinsic value of an additional dollar in terms of a national currency. Authors differ in stressing the welfare, opportunity-cost, or equilibrium characteristics of this shadow exchange rate. In any case, it is considered to be more realistic than the official or market rate of exchange as a standard against which to compare the anticipated net benefit of a proposed investment with respect to its exchange-earning or exchange-saving objectives. A project which would only be profitable at an exchange rate higher than the shadow rate should presumably be rejected as involving a waste of resources.

Attempts to compute shadow rates of exchange as dual variables from formal programming models, taking account of all the relevant constraints and eliminating the distortions introduced by the tariff system into domestic prices, run into difficult technical problems.[18] It is computationally impractical to derive credible results in sufficient industry or commodity detail to say anything very useful about comparative advantage.

A more practical approach is to rank projects according to exporting or import-substituting potential in implicit exchange-rate terms by either of two principal methods. One is by calculation of the domestic-resource cost of foreign exchange for each industry or project, i.e., the exchange rate at which its output would be competitive internationally. This method is best known for its application in Israel by Michael Bruno[19] and in Turkey by Anne O. Krueger.[20] The other method involves calculation of levels of effective protection and converting these into exchange-rate form, i.e., by computing the exchange rates at which the effective rate of protection on each activity would be zero. The significant difference between the two techniques is that the Bruno-Krueger measurement values domestically produced intermediate inputs at domestic prices, whereas the effective-tariff approach prices tradable inputs at international prices. The former has the disadvantage of imposing an unnecessarily stringent test.[21]

Either way of ranking projects gives only the relative scale of resource-cost exchange rates. In order to compare export-promoting or import-substituting projects with purely domestic infrastructure projects, it is necessary to have a general shadow price of foreign exchange to serve as a cutoff criterion, or for imputing world prices to nontraded goods. The preferred method seems to be to use for this purpose the equilibrium (without tariff) exchange rate as in computing net rates of effective protection. As pointed out in Chapter 1, this involves an elaborate calculation using price elasticities for imports and exports, and the results of which would be of only very ephemeral value. Ian M. D. Little and James A. Mirrlees have suggested that for many practical purposes arising in project selection it would suffice to use a standard conversion factor, i. e., a crude average of international price ratios for a representative selection of commodities.[22]

It is apparent that the conceptual framework used in the fields of project selection and evaluation corresponds closely to that used in the analysis of a country's structure of nominal and effective protection, despite differences in terminology.

STATUS OF RESEARCH AND RESEARCH NEEDS

Interest in empirical studies of the relationship between comparative advantage and levels of protection has greatly increased during the past five years or so, accompanying the rapid theoretical development of the concept of effective protection.

Much of this research has been conducted under contract with the U.S. Agency for International Development (AID), such as the series of studies on import substitution and economic policy being produced by the Williams College group of economists[23] under a research program extending from 1964 to 1972. A number of these papers have been cited in the present study. Although much of the Williams group's work has involved case studies of Asian or African countries (Pakistan, the Philippines, and Ghana), the methodologies used are just as applicable to Latin America, and that area is represented by papers on Brazil, Colombia, and Mexico. Mention should also be made of the Harvard program of comparative studies of resource allocation and development policy and other AID-sponsored research at the RAND Corporation, the Yale Economic Growth Center, the University of California, and the University of Wisconsin.

Another important body of research on levels of protection in the context of comparative advantage and industrial development has been carried on by a group of scholars sponsored by the Economic Development Center of the Organization for Economic Cooperation and Development in Paris.[24]

The International Bank for Reconstruction and Development (IBRD), as a major supplier of development finance given on a project-by-project basis, has a particular interest in project-selection methodology, and is now giving increasing attention to the comparative-advantage criterion. Bela Balassa, who played a leading role in the elaboration of the theoretical concept of effective protection, has been in charge of the studies sponsored jointly by the IBRD and the Inter-American Development Bank on effective protection in developing countries.[25] Individual Latin American countries which have been the object of special studies under this project are Brazil (Joel Bergsman), Chile (Teresa Jeanneret), and Mexico (Gerardo Bueno).

Regardless of the particular sponsoring agency, there is considerable overlap, both with respect to country coverage and participating authors, in all these projects, which are in general inspired by the same methodological approach and by the same preoccupation with the resource-allocation effects of protective policies. This research has also had significant impact on thinking in the developing countries under study, including those in Latin America. Such influence has been transmitted through direct collaboration with governmental departments (especially the planning bureaus), universities, and research foundations or institutes in the host countries and through exchange fellowships. The increased awareness and theoretical sophistication in Latin America on the whole subject of protection is particularly noticeable among the rising young economists, many of whom now have responsible positions for practical formulation of commercial policy, while still retaining a foothold in the academic research institutes in their countries.

In Argentina, the current work of the following institutes is especially noteworthy in this domain: Instituto Torcuato di Tella (Centro de Investigaciones Económicas), FIEL (Fundación de Investigaciones Económicas Latinoamericanas), and the Centro de Estudios de Conjuntura of the IDES (Instituto de Desarrollo Económico y Social.) Staff collaborators of these institutions now occupy important positions in the Argentine planning organization (CONADE) and in the economic ministries, where they have direct influence on commercial policy. The Instituto para la Integracion de America Latina (INTAL, sponsored by the Inter-American Development Bank) is also in Buenos Aires. It has carried out and published valuable research on various topics connected with Latin American integration, especially the institutional aspects, including a major statistical project on the role of multinational firms in development of nontraditional exports. Its book on problems of a common external tariff for Latin America contains several important articles on Latin American tariff structure.[26]

The picture is similar in Brazil, where the semiofficial Fundação Getulio Vargas produces a broad spectrum of statistical and analytical work, part of which is relevant to our present concerns. Another organization, the IPEA (Instituto de Pesquisa Econômica-

Social Aplicada) has done work on effective tariffs. Work on effective tariffs is also going forward in the Finance Ministry; the central bank is collecting data on implicit exchange rates.

In Chile, current studies of nominal and effective tariffs have been contracted by the government to the Economic Institute of the Catholic University of Chile. The National Planning Office (ODEPLAN) has produced several monographs on the use and limitations of shadow prices for foreign exchange in connection with project evaluation.[27] Analysis of commercial policy in Chile is of special interest because for some time the Chilean authorities have been preparing for a general reform of the import regime, whereby all types of restrictions would be consolidated on an ad valorem tariff basis as a first step toward eventual rationalization of the nation's chaotic protective system. These studies are being coordinated by the Central Bank.

This illustrative survey of research in Latin America on the allocational aspects of protection cannot ignore the considerable activity in Mexico. The development bank, Nacional Financiera, has sponsored a number of studies in this field. (Gerardo Bueno, who prepared the IBRD country study of Mexican effective protection, is director of industrial programming with that institution.) Victor L. Urquidi, A. Calderón Martínez, O. Campos Salas, and P. García Reynoso are among the Mexican economists in and out of government agencies who have produced important studies of the commercial-policy aspect of development strategy. Miguel S. Wionzcek of the CEMLA (Centro de Estudios Monetarios Latinoamericanos) should also be mentioned in this connection.

The United Nations has been a prolific source of studies on macroeconomic planning and microeconomic project-selection techniques.[28] Besides the Department of Economic and Social Affairs at UN Headquarters, the United Nations Organization for Industrial Development (UNIDO) and particularly the regional economic commissions have been active in these fields. The role of the Economic Commission for Latin America calls for special comment.

ECLA's approach toward development problems has been dominated by its emphasis on balanced growth and quantitative planning techniques, and by a relative lack of interest in questions of comparative advantage. Characteristically, ECLA tends to be pessimistic with respect to prospects for access of Latin American manufactured exports to the markets of industrialized countries. This, combined with a preoccupation with the Prebisch thesis on the external strangulation resulting from a chronic tendency of the terms of trade at the center of the world economy to become more and more unfavorable to Latin America and other countries of the periphery, made the ECLA

Secretariat throw its considerable intellectual influence in Latin America on the side of justifying the import substitution policies of the
1950's.[29] Hollis B. Chenery has pointed out that ECLA's methodology
of development programming introduced comparative advantage only
to a very limited extent.[30]

Given this background, it is all the more significant that it was
ECLA that produced, in 1964, one of the most blistering criticisms
of high and illogical levels of protection in Latin America, pointing
out the adverse effects on efficiency and on Latin America's ability
to export. The article in question, written by Santiago Marcario,
director of ECLA's trade division, also contained the most comprehensive analytical compilation of internationally comparable data on
tariffs and other trade restrictions in developing countries that has
yet been published.[31]

From the beginning of the 1960's, there had been increasing criticism by Prebisch and other ECLA officials of such excessive protection and, more generally, of import substitution at any cost where
this was at the national level.[32] However, because of continued export-
pessimism, exemplified in the trade-gap analysis, which originated
in ECLA and was further developed in UNCTAD, the strategy of import
substitution was not repudiated by ECLA, but simply transferred from
the national to the regional level. The emphasis of the new rationale
was placed more on the need to achieve economies of scale (and, to
a considerable extent, on political considerations) than on the allocational criterion of comparative advantage.

This pattern of though is particularly apparent in the output of
ECLA's affiliated organization, ILPES (Instituto Latinoamericano de
Planificación Económica y Social), which is dominated by the trade-
gap concept and by the quantitative approach to planning. In the impressive ILPES documentation on regional integration, export policy,
macroeconomic planning criteria, cost-benefit analysis for optimal
choice of industries, structural unemployment, industrial capacity,
and growth rates, it is difficult to find even a mention of the levels of
protection in Latin America.[33]

Perhaps because there were other budgetary or administrative
priorities, the ECLA Secretariat has not seen fit to update the valuable
information contained in the 1964 article on the structure of Latin American protection or to follow it up with further analysis comparable to
that now being carried out under other auspices. To be sure, certain
passages in several recent documents on Latin American development
and trade policy do come out against excessive protection, but relatively
little space is devoted to this matter, which is overshadowed by the
strictures aimed at the commercial policies of countries farther North.

One recent ECLA document [34] (written by the former director of
ECLA's Industry Division) is noteworthy for its balanced presentation,
giving adequate attention to the effects of existing levels of protection
on the structural difficulties of Latin American industry in the context
of efforts to pursue regional integration objectives and taking account
of supply as well as demand aspects of promoting manufactured exports
to the rest of the world. The appearance of this study under the ECLA
imprint justifies hope that the organization will pick up where it left
off in 1964 and will again contribute constructively to the diagnosis
and therapy of Latin American protectionism.

From this sampling of recent and current research on the use
of levels of protection in assessing comparative advantage, it can be
concluded that there is no lack of theoretical analysis or of experi-
mentation with programming models. However, at the level of
practical application of these techniques, especially in the field of
cost-benefit analysis for project selection in the light of comparative advantage, there is still much to be desired, mainly because of the
the lack of usable statistical data on protection.

Specifically, the area in which data are most lacking is in the
measurement of international price disparities, which define the
levels of actual nominal protection and without which no reliable ap-
praisal of comparative advantage can be made either in terms of
Corden-Johnson-Balassa effective protection or in terms of Bruno-
Krueger-Lewis implicit exchange rates. Such information is needed
both at a disaggregated industry or product level and in broader aggregates. Although data-collection and methodological problems are involved, they are similar to those arising in making other kinds of
price-index numbers from samplings of price relatives. Preferably,
such international price comparisons should be made on a systematic
and continuing basis so as to yield time series. Product classifications
should be such as can be linked conveniently to tariff schedules, trade
statistics, and input-output and industrial-census nomenclatures.

Ultimately and ideally, this effort should be part of the normal
statistical program of national statistical offices. Meanwhile, there
are various avenues toward a partial fulfillment of the requirement
that can be explored further.

First, as far as final products (consumer and capital goods) are
concerned, it has been seen that price ratios measured for purposes
of comparing real-income levels provide a proxy for the price ratios
needed for measuring the nominal protection and effective protection
and comparative advantage, to the extent that the items sampled are
either imported or compete with imported goods. The market-basket

data for the ECLA real-income study are now almost ten years out of date. However, new bench-mark data will soon be available from the new studies being carried out under the Brookings ECIEL project on international prices and real-income comparisons in which is to be linked with similar data from other parts of the world under the coordination of the UN Statistical Office.

A start has been made on collecting another body of international price comparisons by the National Bureau of Economic Research.[35] material may be useful in providing basic data and methods for evaluating the intermediate products not covered by the price comparisons for final goods used in real-income studies.

Finally, following the suggestion of George B. Baldwin of the World Bank, it would be better than nothing if that or a similar agency concerned with project-selection problems were simply

> to build up and maintain a file of comparative advantage figures as an aid to decision making by government agencies, development banks, tariff commissions, and other bodies. One could begin by collecting cif price quotations for a manageable list of commonly imported items. Within a few months one or two energetic and resourceful junior research officers could set up files on perhaps 50, 75 products. Most of the information would have to be collected by talking with importers, foreign sales representatives in the country, and purchasing officers. The research department of a development bank is probably the most promising place to have this work done, though certainly not the only one. . . . From such an effort there would emerge, quite quickly, a rough standard for judging whether or not a particular industry looked like an attractive use of the country's resources.[36]

NOTES

1. See Gottfried Haberler, A Survey of International Trade Theory (International Finance Section, Princeton University, Special Papers in International Economics, No. 1, July, 1961, pp. 6-23.) For popularized versions, see George B. Baldwin, ' 'What Price Domestic Industry ?'' Finance and Development, III, 1 (March, 1966), 24-30, and Leland B. Yeager and David G. Tuerck, Trade Policy and the Price System (Scranton, Pa. : International Textbook Co., 1966), pp. 31-67.

2. Hollis B. Chenery, "Comparative Advantage and Development Policy", American Economic Review, LI, 1 (March, 1961), 19.

3.   Eli Heckscher, "The Effect of Foreign Trade on the Distribution of Income," reprinted in Readings in the Theory of International Trade, op. cit.,pp. 272-300.

4.   See Lloyd A. Metzler, "The Theory of International Trade,"
in Howard S. Ellis, ed., A Survey of Contemporary Economics, Vol. 1
(Homewood, Illinois. Richard D. Irwin, Inc., fifth printing, 1956),
pp. 244-49; citations listed by Chenery, op. cit., and the extensive
literature on the "Leontief Paradox."

5.   Hal B. Lary, Imports of Manufactures from Less Developed
Countries (National Bureau of Economic Research, Inc., Columbia
University Press, 1968).

6.   Daniel M. Schydlowsky, "Analytical Basis for a National
Policy on Regional Economic Integration in Latin America," Journal
of Common Market Studies, VI, 2 (December, 1967), 179-96.

7.   Ian Little, Tibor Scitovsky, and Maurice Scott, Industry
and Trade in Some Developing Countries: A Comparative Study.
(London, Oxford University Press, 1970), p. 190.

8.   Harry G. Johnson, "The Costs of Protection and Self Suffi-
ciency," Quarterly Journal of Economics, 79, 4 (August, 1965), 371.

9.   Arnold C. Harberger, "Using the Resources at Hand More
Effectively," American Economic Review, Papers and Proceedings,
XLIX, 2 (May, 1959), 134-55.

10.   Bela Balassa "Resource Allocation and Economic Integration in Latin America" (Conference at Cornell University on
"The Next Decade of Latin American Development," April 20-22,
1966) (mimeograph--revised), p. 7.

11.   Several specific case studies are discussed in Little,
Scitovsky, and Scott, op. cit., pp. 190-97.

12.   Bela Balassa, Trade Liberalization Among Industrial
Countries: Objectives and Alternatives (New York: McGraw-Hill Book
Co., 1967), pp. 86-92.

13.   Herbert G. Grubel, "Intra-Industry Specialization and the
Pattern of Trade," Canadian Journal of Economics and Political
Science, 33, 3 (August, 1967), 374-88.

14.   Roy F. Harrod, International Economics (Chicago: University
of Chicago Press, rev. ed., 1957), pp. 53-57.

15. A. R. Prest and R. Turvey, "Cost-Benefit Analysis: A Survey," The Economic Journal (December, 1965),pp. 683-735. (Bibliography contains 90 items.)

16. See Robert Dorfman, Paul A. Samuelson, and Robert M. Solow, Linear Programming and Economic Analysis (New York: McGraw-Hill Book Co., 1958), pp. 59-62.

17. Jan Tinbergen, The Design of Development (Baltimore, 1958), p. 39, quoted in Chenery, op. cit., p. 33. The Tinbergen version of the concept has been called "utterly unreal and otherworldly" as a policy guide by Gunnar Myrdal in Asian Drama, A Twentieth Century Fund Study (New York: Pantheon, 1968), pp. 2031-39.

18. Edmar Bacha and Lance Taylor, Foreign Exchange Shadow Prices in Chile: Conflicting Theories and Comparative Evaluations (Santiago: Oficina de Planificación Nacional, October, 1969), pp. 4-6, 32-34.

19. Michael Bruno, "The Optimal Selection of Export-Promoting and Import-Substituting Projects," in United Nations, Planning and the External Sector: Techniques, Problems and Policies, Report of the First Interregional Seminar on Development Planning, Ankara, Turkey, September 6-17, 1965. (New York: United Nations, 1967)

20. Anne O. Krueger, "Some Economic Costs of Exchange Control, The Turkish Case," Journal of Political Economy, LXXIV, 5 (October, 1966), 466-80.

21. Bela Balassa and Daniel M. Schydlowsky, "Effective Tariffs, Domestic Cost of Foreign Exchange, and the Equilibrium Exchange Rate," Journal of Political Economy (May-June, 1968), pp. 348-60.

22. Ian M. D. Little and James A. Mirrlees, "Social Cost-Benefit Analysis," Manual of Industrial Project Analysis in Developing Countries (Paris: Development Center of the OECD, 1969), Vol. II.

23. Henry J. Bruton, Paul G. Clark, Stephen R. Lewis, Jr., John H. Power, John B. Sheahan, William F. Steel, Gordon C. Winston, et al. For a concise review of the findings of this project to date, see Henry J. Bruton, The Import Substitution Strategy of Economic Development: A Survey of Findings, Research Memorandum No. 27 (Williamstown, Mass.: Center for Development Economics, Williams College, April, 1969).

24. Little, Scitovsky, and Scott, op. cit., contains the overall findings. Country studies on Brazil (Joel Bergsman), Mexico (Timothy King), and four non-Latin American countries are being published as separate books.

25. Bela Balassa and Associates, The Structure of Protection in Developing Countries (Baltimore: Johns Hopkins Press, 1971).

26. Hacia una Tarifa Externa Común en America Latina (Buenos Aires: INTAL, 1969).

27. Bacha and Taylor, op. cit. See also E. R. Fontaine, El Precio sombra de las Divisas para le Evaluación Social de Projectos (Santiago: Universidad Católica de Chile, 1969).

28. See United Nations, Department of Economic and Social Affairs, ''Annotated Bibliography of Major United Nations Publications and Documents on Development Planning, 1955-1968, '' Journal of Development Planning (Sales No. E.69.II.B 24), pp. 173-208.

29. Werner Baer, '' The Economics of Prebisch and ECLA, '' in Charles T. Nisbet, ed., Latin America: Problems in Economic Development (New York: Free Press, 1969), pp. 203-18; Raúl Prebisch, ''The Economic Development of Latin America and Its Principal Problems'' (Santiago, 1950), reprinted in Economic Bulletin for Latin America, VII, 1 (1962), 1-22.

30. Chenery, op. cit., p. 44.

31. Santiago Macario, '' Protectionism and Industrialization In Latin America, Economic Bulletin for Latin America, IX, 1 (March, 1964), 61-101. See especially p. 77.

32. [Raúl Prebisch] Towards a Dynamic Development Policy for Latin America (New York: United Nations, 1963, E/CN. 12/680/ Rev. 1), pp. 67-73.

33. See for examples: ILPES, La Brecha Comercial y la Integración Lationoamericana (Mexico: Siglo Ventiuno Editores S.A., 1967).

34. ECLA, The United Nations Second Development Decade: Industrial Development in Latin America (E/CN. 12/830, March 13, 1969). See especially pp. 68-73, 77, 118, 153-55.

35. Irving B. Kravis and Robert E. Lipsey, Measuring International Price Competitiveness: A Preliminary Report, National Bureau of Economic Research (NBER) (Occasional Paper 94, 1965), and Comparative Prices of Nonferrous Metals in International Trade, 1953-64 (Occasional Paper 98, 1966). Further exploitation of this data will be embodied in a forthcoming NBER study on the role of prices in international trade.

36. Baldwin, op. cit., pp. 29-30

6

IMPORT SUBSTITUTION VS. IMPORT-SUBSTITUTION POLICIES

The purpose of this chapter is to identify certain more or less common characteristics of Latin American import-substitution policy revealed by the analysis of profiles of protection.

The import-substitution type of commercial policy, as a so-called strategy of development, is obviously not limited to Latin America, but is found in many developing and, especially, semi-industrialized countries in other parts of the world. However, the Latin American countries, having attained political independence a century and a half ago, have had a much longer period than Asian and African countries in which to follow monetary, exchange, and commercial policies in the name of nationally sovereign objectives, unrestrained by colonial preferential systems or by membership in monetary blocs like the Sterling Area and the Franc Zone. Moreover, although the policies of the Latin American countries were adopted in uncoordinated fashion, mainly under the pressure of events in the 1930's and 1940's, a relatively coherent body of doctrine and systematic analysis of import substitution appeared first in the publications of the Economic Commission for Latin America.

One should not confuse import-substitution policy with import substitution as such. It is possible for either one to exist without the other. Some import substitution always accompanies industrial development,[1] even when this is based on relatively outward-looking commercial policies[2] or on charges in comparative advantage.[3] On the other hand, it is well known that, when import-substitution policy is pushed beyond a certain point, it is ultimately self-frustrating: the import coefficient (ratio of total imports to total supply) can no longer be compressed, and substitution of imports of finished goods tends to be more and more offset by increased imports of components for assembly, raw materials, other intermediate goods, and capital goods.[4]

The definition of import substitution per se has evolved considerably since Hollis B. Chenery's article, which defined it simply as the reduction in the fraction of total supply attributed to imports.[5]

The Latin American Institute for Social and Economic Planning (ILPES) uses a very complicated definition, taking account of the changes in structure of imports accompanying the industrialization process and of the changes in demand, taking as point of reference an imaginary situation in which substitution policies are neutral, and recognizing the tendency toward exhaustion of import substitution.[6] Celso Furtado defines import substitution as the increase in the industrial production destined for the internal market taken as a proportion of GDP when the proportion of imports to GDP is declining.[7]

While such definitions are necessary for analytical purposes such as measuring the role of import substitution in growth, etc., they tell nothing about casual relationships. In fact, observed import substitution as measured by the decline in the proportion of demand met by imports might be the result, rather than the cause, of industrial development. A distinction should therefore be made between spontaneous import substitution associated with shifts in demand, changing factor proportions, improved technology, etc., on the one hand, and conscious efforts at replacing imports through imposition of protective measures, on the other. Import-substitution policies may not only sometimes have adverse effects on economic development through long-run effects on incentives and productivity, they may also have perverse short-term effects on observed import substitution itself.

It is with these policies that the rest of this chapter is concerned. First, however, we consider one attempt that has been made to reconcile import-substitution policy with the criterion of comparative advantage, and which, at the same time, deals with the infant-industry argument for protection in terms consistent with the concepts of the present study.

Stephen R. Lewis, Jr.,[8] has defined "successful" import substitution as having been attained when the domestic price (and cost) of a commodity falls, because of economies of scale or whatever reason, to such an extent that the relationship between the domestic and foreign price (cif) is below the implicit exchange rate defined by the official exchange rate adjusted for the tariff. The legal tariff therefore becomes in part redundant. At a still later stage of "success," the international price relationship becomes equal to the official exchange

rate, so that the country can begin to export the product--that is, the
tariff is completely redundant and can be abolished. It may be too
harsh a test that this should occur at official exchange rates (implying
an absolute advantage). From a comparative advantage standpoint,
it is sufficient that the internal price fall sufficiently so that the international price relationship will be equal to or less than the equilibrium
(without tariff) exchange rate.

EXPORT-DISINCENTIVE EFFECTS OF
TARIFF STRUCTURE

If nominal protection on a given product is defined in terms of
the disparity between its domestic and foreign price, and if there are
no taxes or subsidies on its exportation, the height of the (nonredundant)
nominal tariff measures the country's absolute disadvantage in the
export of that product at the given exchange rate. There is obviously
a strong disincentive against exporting if all that is obtained as proceeds
is the local countervalue at the official rate of exchange, when the
same product could be sold on the local market at the higher protected
price determined by the countervalue of the official rate plus the
tariff.

To measure this disincentive effect, as far as a manufacturer
is concerned, the calculation must also allow for the cost of inputs.
Thus, Balassa defines discrimination in favor of import substitution
and against exportation as the percentage difference between the
value added obtained from production for the home market and that
obtained from exporting.[9] Where exporters enjoy no privileged access
to raw materials and intermediate goods, the relative bias against
exports in different industries depends on the difference between the
nominal protection and the rate of export subsidy received on each
industry's output; it also depends on the varying extent to which the
cost of each industry's inputs is raised by tariffs, etc., over what the
inputs would have cost under free trade. To the extent that exporters
enjoy free-trade-zone privileges, obtain customs drawbacks, or are
allocated special import quotas for their input requirements, the
discrimination against exporting is reduced.

Some discrimination against exporting is normal in all countries
that derive fiscal revenue from foreign trade, whether it is imports
or exports that are taxed. (In this connection, one may recall Abba
Lerner's "symmetry" theorem on the equivalence of both kinds of
taxes on trade,[10] which can be extended to cover differentiated tariff
structures and to take account of intermediate products.[11])

Export taxes are usually applied by Latin American countries

on those traditional primary export products on which they expect to
be able to affect the terms of trade, e.g., Brazilian and Colombian
coffee, Chilean copper, Venezuelan petroleum, and Argentine meat
and grain. Such export taxes also are frequently intended to have an
income-redistributive fiscal effect; they may have a political background,
especially where foreign capital plays an important role in their
production. Whether or not the terms of trade can be manipulated
by imposing an export tax, by avoiding a devaluation that would be
justified on other grounds, or by quantitatively limiting exports, depends
not only on the price elasticity of foreign demand, but also on the
supply elasticity at home and abroad. Disregard of foreign supply
elasticity has probably led some Latin American countries to suffer
a permanent loss of market shares in favor of other producing countries.
While a systematic policy of discrimination against traditional low-
elasticity exports may be justified, not only for direct terms-of-trade
reasons, but also for the sake of export diversification away from
overdependence on products that are subject to wide fluctuations of
world price and supply or for which international demand shows little
long-term growth, countries often overestimate their power over the
market for their major exports. Meanwhile, they are likely also to
be penalizing their nontraditional exports through having extremely
high import tariffs that are only partially offset by export subsidies.

The problem of the discrimination against exporting that is
embodied in an import-substitution-oriented tariff structure gets all
mixed up, analytically, with problems of domestic monetary policy
and policy with respect to the exchange rate. Until the recent reem-
phasis on tariff theory, most writers stressed mainly domestic inflation, insufficient supply, high absolute-wage costs, high input costs,
low labor productivity, etc., in explaining why many Latin American
countries are priced out of the market as far as nontraditional exports
are concerned. Or the full blame may be placed on protectionist
measures or alleged dumping practices of the industrialized countries.
All these factors may well belong in the model, but there has probably
been insufficient attention paid to the price-distorting role of the
structure of protection. An important aspect of the latter has been
the tendency of countries to try to put the burden of balance-of-payments
adjustment entirely on imports--via the protective system--instead
of dividing it more symmetrically between imports and exports--via
exchange-rate modification. High levels of nominal protection on
intermediate goods account for most of the high cost of inputs, and
high tariffs on final products lead to a high rate of domestic absorption
of potential exports except where there is no inflationary excess demand
and where there is sufficient domestic competition and productivity
growth for the tariffs to become significantly redundant. A cross-
country analysis by Barend A. De Vries has shown that the growth
performance of minor exports tends to be poor in countries with

relatively strong inflation.[12] Although De Vries stressed the negative
influence of inward-orientation policies on the performance of nontraditional exports, he made no attempt to use this factor of protectionist
policy as an explanatory variable in his regressions. This is unfortu-
nate, because one suspects that this might have given a better fit than
his inflation variable, which did not give significant coefficients in all
the regression equations. In any case, the rates of inflation in Latin
American countries appear to have been correlated with average
levels of protection. There are various models of the mechanism of
inflation that would explain this association. Baldinelli stresses the
conflict among the various economic sectors and special interests to
increase their respective shares in the national income. After a
devaluation, a large part of a high tariff becomes redundant, giving
scope for substantial price increases unchecked by external competition.[13]
The import-substitutive structure of protection also plays a role--
although apparently a minor one--among other "structural" factors
in Furtado's analysis of the inflationary process.[14]

Several UNCTAD studies have been concerned, as was De Vries',
with cross-country comparisons of performance of developing countries
with respect to export of manufactures.[15] Cross-country multiple
regressions were run in the attempt to analyze variations in the per
capita exports of a large number of countries in terms of various
explanatory variables, but not including protectionist policy, unfortunately. In each of these studies, the strongly import-substitutive
Latin American countries other than Mexico showed large unexplained
negative residuals. Again, there seems to be little doubt that inclusion
of an indicator of inward-looking policy would have greatly improved
the analysis and raised the coefficient of determination (R^2). It is
curious that in the recent UNCTAD study, no consideration whatsoever
was given to this factor of commercial-policy discrimination against
exporting.

Import substitution and discouragement of exports are thus two
sides of a coin. In view of the universal prevalence of mercantilistic
attitudes, such extreme discrimination against exporting as was found
over a number of years in several South American countries seems
sufficiently unusual to warrant further consideration of the probable
motives. Nathaniel Leff has attributed the antiexport orientation of
Brazil and certain other countries, including Argentina and Colombia,
to an exportable-surplus attitude toward trade:

> Following this approach, a country exports only the "surplus"
> which is "left-over" after the domestic market has been
> "adequately" supplied. Domestic demand takes priority,
> however, and must be supplied even if internal prices are
> lower than world market prices.[16]

To be sure, this approach relates mainly to traditional exports, the
foreign demand for which is assumed to be price-inelastic anyway,
so that the withholding of potential exports may seem to coincide with
the country's terms-of-trade interest. Other rationalizations of the
exportable-surplus attitude, as it concerns traditional, nonmanufactured
goods, are sociopolitical (to weaken the power of the landowners and
exporter-capitalists)[17] or counterinflationary (since many of these
products, e.g., meat in Argentina, are important wage-goods).

Perhaps equally important in inhibiting export promotion has
been an attitude of export pessimism. As applied to foodstuffs, this
is rooted in the doctrine, based on Engel's Law, that low income
elasticity of demand for most of these products puts a ceiling on their
exportation to the industrialized countries. This argument, of course,
does not apply to manufactured goods and nontraditional agricultural
exports. Although some writers speak of an internally determined
export maximum for manufactures (determined by immobility of production factors, lack of sufficient domestic market, etc.),[18] the main
emphasis has been placed on the trade restrictions of the developed
countries. In that connection, the escalation of nominal and effective
protection has been stressed as a major barrier frustrating access
for those labor-intensive goods in the production of which developing
countries are believed to have a comparative advantage.[19] One can
debate whether the import tariffs of the industrial countries, at post-
Kennedy Round levels, actually constitute a greater impediment to
Latin American exports of processed goods than the price effects of
Latin American protectionism.* Mexico's success in rapidly expanding
and diversifying its manufactured exports can not be ignored, even by
export pessimists. On the other hand, the public statements of labor
leaders, industrialists, legislators, and officials in the United States,
together with the increasing recourse to imposition of "voluntary"
controls on imports, tend to give credence to the notion that there is
such a tight ceiling on the capacity of developed countries to absorb
labor-intensive manufactured exports from developing countries
that it would be futile for the latter to attempt to break out of their
import-substituting and export-discouraging straitjackets. This
implication is pointed up in the following example cited by the secre-
tary-general of the Central American Common Market.

---

*Regression analysis indicates that Latin American countries
face income and price elasticities of foreign demand quite favorable
for expansion of their manufactured exports, but exporters in countries
whose policies discriminate most against exports respond poorly to
price incentives. (Henry J. Bruton, Latin American Exports and
Import Substitution Policies, [Research Memorandum No. 32, Center
for Development Economics, Williams College, July 1968], pp. 24-27.)

> An illustration . . . is the case of a Central American
> country which has set up a plant that so far this year has
> exported 1,600 dozen raincoats outside the region. Now a
> request has been made to limit these exports through the
> imposition of a voluntary quota. The example cited is
> only the last in a long series which we are encountering.[20]

This example, among others, is no doubt discouraging, but
countries in other parts of the world face the same barriers and
still succeed in increasing their manufactured exports. Between
1964 and 1968 the proportion of manufactures (SITC's 5 to 8 in U.S.
imports from primary-commodity-exporting countries rose from 17
to 24 per cent.[21] The only major Latin American country that participated in this improvement was Mexico, which has relatively little
bias against exporting built into its protective structure.

There are two ways in which the discrimination against exports
(especially nontraditional exports) can be corrected: devaluation or
export subsidization. The best way would clearly be through a compensated devaluation, consisting of a combination of devaluation and
changes in nominal tariffs (including other trade taxes and subsidies)
so designed as to leave unchanged, or at least to minimize, changes
in domestic prices and in effective protection on imports. The basic
rate for conversion of export proceeds would presumably be raised
in this process to a sufficiently high level to eliminate most of the
discrimination against nontraditional exports. Meanwhile, either a
separate exchange rate or an export tax could be applied to those
traditional or "strong" exports for which the price elasticity of foreign
demand and foreign supply was considered to be relatively low. At a
later stage it would be desirable to have further tariff reform (possibly combined with a further exchange-rate reform) so as to smooth
out the profile of import protection. For purposes of reducing discrimination against exporting, however, the most important step is
the absorption of as much of the tariff into the exchange rate as is
possible without setting off adverse domestic repercussions such as
new impulses toward cost-push inflation.

A scientifically designed compensated devaluation is probably
too much to ask of policy makers in a practical political situation.
The next-best course of action might be any reasonably-well-imple-
mented policy of exchange-rate adjustment cum tariff reform to
eliminate overvaluation, while at the same time keeping tariffs from
moving up with the exchange rate. (It is important to prevent appearance of a wide new margin of tariff redundancy that would invite further
price increases in monopolistic industries.) Reference to Chart 4
("Profiles of Implicit Exchange Rates: Argentina, 1965 and 1967")
and to Chart 16 ("Brazil: Nominal Protection--Profiles of Implicit

Exchange Rates, by use classes, 1953-67") will show how Argentina and Brazil, respectively, eliminated at least some of their discrimination against nontraditional exporting by their exchange cum tariff reforms of 1967. Recent trade data indicate that the export competitiveness of both countries has greatly improved as a result of these reforms. An important difference between the two cases is that the Argentine devaluation left a relatively larger degree of discrimination against exporting. Moreover, the Argentine devaluation was intended to be a once-and-for-all measure, which put a greater burden on internal anti-inflationary policy than in the case of Brazil, where the series of frequent subsequent devaluations has kept the basic exchange rate from falling too far behind the rise in internal prices.

It may be noted parenthetically that in those countries where there are frequent adjustments of the exchange rate (Brazil and Chile) it is probably easier to reform the tariff structure than in countries, like Mexico, which enjoy greater stability.

> The main exchange maladjustments in non-export activities tend to be reflected in the tariff, while those maladjust-. ments involving exporting are reflected in the exchange rate. At the same time, however, the unstable countries are also those most accustomed to changes in cost structures, since inflation does not affect all sectors equally or simultaneously. The tendency toward upward leveling means that readjustments are continuous when inflation and devaluations are "secular." On the other hand, the political effort needed to effect structural changes must be greater in those countries where the population is not accustomed to change than in those where it is. In this sense, it could be more difficult politically (meet more resistance) to effect the readjustment resulting from a decrease of 10 per cent in the Mexican or Guatemalan tariff than from a 50 per cent decrease in the tariff of Brazil or Chile.[22]

The only alternative to devaluation cum tariff reduction is export subsidization, if it is desired to reduce the discrimination against exporting. The variety of possible types of export subsidies is manifold, as reported in a recent UNCTAD study.[23] Incentives in the context of exchange rates include currency retention schemes, export bonus/import entitlement schemes, special import licenses for exporters, foreign exchange allocations to exporters, and multiple exchange-rate systems. Among those levies which might be exempted or remitted are single- and multiple-stage production and sales taxes, import duties, and export taxes. Income taxes could be alleviated by export rebates (in relation to size of income or profit from exports, growth in income from exports, or size and growth in level of income from exports), export promotional cost rebates, tax-free reserve funds, accelerated depreciation and investment allowances, and tax holidays. (In addition, the UNCTAD document lists various types of "input incentives" and "government market assistance and other services" for exporters; these categories have probably less or no direct effects on export prices at the margin, and can therefore be disregarded for present purposes.)

At present, Venezuela is the only Latin American country using a special exchange rate, more favorable than the basic rate, to promote certain exports (coffee and cocoa). Exemption or remission of domestic indirect taxes is practiced only by Argentina, Brazil, and Ecuador. Argentina, Brazil, Colombia, Mexico, and Peru give certain income tax rebates or other income tax advantages to exporters. Certain export duties are rebated or exempted for specified products in Brazil, Bolivia, Ecuador, Mexico, Paraguay, and Peru. (This can hardly be considered export subsidization; it merely moderates a penalty on certain exports.) Concessions are made to exporters on certain minor taxes in Brazil, Chile, Ecuador, and Peru. Drawbacks of import duties exist in Argentina, Brazil, Chile, and Mexico, while exemptions, temporary-entry, and bonded-zone arrangements of varying degrees of coverage are applied in Argentina, Brazil, Chile, Colombia, Ecuador, Mexico, and Panama (but apparently not in Paraguay, Peru, Uruguay, or Venezuela).[24]

Although when compared with developing countries in other parts of the world and with many industrial countries, Latin American countries cannot be said to be making excessive use of export-subsidization techniques; furthermore, recourse to drawbacks and to reimbursement or exemption of indirect taxes seem to be on the increase. This would appear to reflect a welcome rise in export-consciousness and a diminution of export pessimism.

One major disadvantage of export subsidization, compared with devaluation, as a means of reducing the discrimination against exporting implicit in an import-substitutive protective structure, is that it is more or less illegal in GATT (Article 16). In some cases it can expose the offending country to countervailing and antidumping duties. If it were strictly applied to most Latin American countries (which has not been the case) the General Agreement on Tariffs and Trade (GATT) rule would seem rather unfair, since the subsidization usually offsets only a portion of the exporter's price handicap resulting from protection and currency overvaluation. To be sure, a country is theoretically free to avoid the need for subsidies simply by absorbing tariffs into the exchange rate, but devaluation usually involves a hard political decision that no policymaker is likely to make until long after it is overdue.

        Aside from the pragmatic objection that special export incentives
may attract more or less justified complaints from trading partners
(e.g., the U.S.-Brazilian imbroglio over soluble coffee), or even run
afoul of countervailing duties, they are criticized by economic theorists
on the same grounds that high import duties are criticized: because,
being differentiated by product, they "imply undesirable and inefficient
discrimination and open the door to full-fledged exchange control."[25]
On the other hand, the more freely a country uses export subsidies
to offset the effects of its protectionism (i.e., the more symmetrical
the system becomes with respect to both imports and exports), the
more the corresponding import tariffs and export subsidies look like
an exchange rate, until--at a certain point--the institutional framework of the system becomes so irrelevant that it can be absorbed by
a devaluation with little difficulty.*

DISCRIMINATION AGAINST PRIMARY PRODUCTION

        The protective profiles of the industrial countries are character-
ized by high protection of agriculture, especially exemplified in the
EEC (Chart 1). The opposite tends to occur in the case of the Latin
American countries following import-substitution policies.

        To be sure, there may be high duties on primary agricultural
products in the tariff schedule, but these are redundant and merely
reflect the lack of logic of tariff-making. (If it occurred to anyone to
import chilled beef into Argentina from outside LAFTA, he would have
to pay a 70 per cent tariff; Uruguay would charge a specific duty
equivalent to 29 per cent ad valorem plus an exchange surcharge of
225 per cent, making a total apparent rate of 254 per cent.) Therefore,
to calculate the discrimination against agriculture, as reflected, for
example, in the internal terms of trade as between agriculture and

---

        *"I think that there are overwhelming arguments in support of
formal parity changes as distinct from equivalent measures involving
tariff plus export subsidies. However, insofar as it is considered
impolitic to resort to frequent parity changes, tariffs and export
subsidies ought to be considered as useful second-best-methods
(superior to quota regimes) of achieving transitions from one parity
to another, precisely because they are more freely employed."
(Jagdish Bhagwati, The Theory and Practice of Commercial Policy:
Departures from Unified Exchange [Princeton, N. J.: International
Finance Section, Special Papers in International Economics, No. 8,
January, 1968] , p. 64.)

manufactures in general, or as between agricultural outputs and inputs for agriculture, it is necessary to use direct price observations or an appropriate proxy therefor, such as the domestic support prices for the agricultural products.

To give a crude illustration: taking the Chilean price of wheat as $82 per ton and the world price (cif) as $75 per ton, the implicit price ratio was about 1.1. This compared with ipr's of 1.7 for agricultural equipment, of 2.8 for fertilizer, and of 2.8 for an unweighted average of 300 (mainly industrial) sample products. In Chile, therefore, the internal terms of trade were very unfavorable to wheat (e.g., 1.1/2.8 = 0.39). In Ecuador, on the other hand, the ipr for wheat was about 1.4, as compared with about 1.3 for agricultural equipment, about 1.4 for fertilizer, and about 1.8 for the unweighted average of the 300 products. Thus, there was some discrimination of the general Ecuadorean tariff structure against wheat, but this was apparently mitigated by low duties on agricultural imports.

Balassa and Associates[26] have contrasted the relatively small amount of discrimination against agriculture in Mexico and Malaya with the very pronounced bias in Chile and Pakistan and have noted that the different evolutions of per-capita food production are about as might be expected in view of the differences in price incentives. In Brazil, on the other hand, agricultural output has progressed despite existence of a substantial relative-price disincentive.

Brazil and Chile have kept prices of agricultural foodstuffs down mainly for anti-inflationary reasons. Colombian, Venezuelan, and Mexican prices for major staples have been fixed relatively higher to encourage increased supply and use of purchased inputs to stimulate productivity.[27] As for Argentina, studies cited by Theodore Schultz stress the stagnation of agriculture in the Pampas, where prices were manipulated downward during the 1940's and 1950's, as contrasted with the situation outside the Pampas, where there were fair incentives to increase output of particular crops for domestic consumption.[28] Schultz has been particularly critical of the disincentive effect of the Chilean imbalance of relative prices with respect to agriculture.

The whole problem of inadequate domestic agricultural price incentives in developing countries received increasing attention several years ago, when excitement over the world food problem was almost equal to that recently displayed over the ecological and environmental problems.

It is popular in Latin America to blame agricultural price disincentives on the availability of U.S. surpluses under P.L. 480 and on the subsidization of exports of farm products under the EEC's common

agricultural policy. Whatever may have been the role of the farm-
support policies of the industrial countries in depressing the world-
market terms of trade against agriculture, the additional depression
of the domestic terms of trade* against agriculture in certain Latin
American countries apparently reflected conscious policy, for which
development economists have long supplied various theoretical justi-
fications.

Aside from the intuitive feeling that a steel mill is representative
of a higher level of economic development than a wheat field, there is
considerable evidence that real output per head generally tends to be
higher in manufacturing than in agriculture. Although this generalization may be a good argument for encouraging industry, it is not necessarily an argument for discouraging agriculture (witness the fact that
the United States and Canada have both steel mills and wheat fields).
In any case, the weight of economic theory holds that protectionist
trade measures are inferior to domestic subsidies for developing
infant industries and for creating external economies and "linkages."

A related rationalization for discriminating against agriculture
and other nonprotected sectors permits the domestic manufacturers
to earn high profits, out of which will flow incremental savings for
investment in industrial growth. Eventually, it is hoped agriculture
will also benefit indirectly. The counter-argument to this is that, if
excessive industrial protection feeds the inflationary process or if
welfare loss from protection is too great in the static or efficiency
sense, much of the incremental savings may prove illusory. Realism
requires an admission, however, that some relative discrimination
against primary production is implicit in any industrialization program;
the question is ultimately one of degree.

There is an extensive literature dealing with the problem of
"alleged distortions in the labour market which produce a disequilib-
rium characterized by an excess of the marginal product of labour in
industry over its marginal product in agriculture."[29] This is the

---

*Domestic terms of trade can be analyzed between regions
(see Chapter 7) of a country or between economic sectors. Such
analysis should be linked to the external terms of trade, since the
domestic and external terms of trade may reinforce or offset each
other. Divergence between the two indicates the degree to which protectionist measures or domestic policies distort price signals given
by the world market. (See Carlos F. Díaz-Alejandro, "An Interpretation
of Argentina's Economic Growth Since 1930," Parts 1 and 2, Journal
of Development Studies [October, 1966, and January, 1967].)

so-called Manoilesco argument, which has numerous derivative
versions.[30] This debate is too esoteric to enter into here. Perhaps
it can be disposed of with the following comment by Bacha and Taylor:

> In Latin America (and in many other countries as well)
> the price distortions between tradable and non-tradable
> goods caused by tariffs and other trade restrictions
> appear to be worse than distortions within the non-
> tradable sector caused by surplus labor.[31]

STEEP ESCALATION

It was brought out in Chapter 1 that escalation of the levels of
protection by ascending stages of production, i.e., from raw materials
through intermediate goods to final goods, is an almost universal
characteristic of tariff systems and that the escalation of the profile
of nominal protection is usually leveraged up still further in the profile
of effective protection of value added (cf. Chart 15). To be sure, escalation of nominal protection does not necessarily result in more than proportional escalation of effective protection. This is because, when raw
materials are imported at world prices, some escalation of nominal
tariff rates would be needed in order just to achieve uniform effective
rates at the higher stages and to avoid backward escalation.

Since the commerical policy of the import-substitutive Latin
American countries gives priority to the promotion of domestic manufacture of final consumer goods, it is natural to expect a steeper pro-
gression of escalation than in the industrial countries. However, the
arithmetic of effective protection was not always as well understood
as it is today. This may explain why there are numerous cases of
backward escalation of effective protection in Latin American tariff
structures. Nevertheless, as a general rule, when Latin American
tariff profiles escalate, they do so with vengeance, and it is likely
that escalation will be more consistently applied in the future than in
the past.

The Argentine tariff reform of 1967 presents a good example of
deliberate escalation policy. Nominal tariff rates were assigned
according to three criteria:
  1. The "degree of processing," measured by value added, rising
along a relative scale of one to ten;
  2. The nature of the goods, whether inputs, consumer goods,
or capital goods; and
  3. The presence or absence of domestic production of the goods
or their substitutes.
Application of these criteria resulted in the basic scheme shown in

Table 7. Although the Argentine tariff system built on this framework
has the virtue of much more logical consistency than the system it
replaced, it can be seen that this pattern of two-way escalation, in
conjunction with the local production criterion, could theoretically
yield effective rates of protection ranging from well below zero to
several hundred percentage points on the positive side. This contrasts
with the policy prescription found in the OECD Development Center's
study of industrialization in developing countries, which concluded
that it was "hard to believe that an average level of more than 20 per
cent could possibly be justified even in the least developed countries."[32]
To obtain uniform effective rates at about that level would require only
very gradual escalation of very moderate nominal tariffs.

From the formula for effective rates of protection, it is apparent
that higher effective rates on outputs can be obtained as well by lowering
nominal tariffs on inputs as by raising nominal tariffs on outputs. This
could even involve subsidization of imports of intermediate goods, so
as to make possible export of final products while giving the domestic
processor substantial effective protection on his activity.[33] Thus,
the protectiveness of the tariff structure can be increased as the result
of lowering nominal tariffs on inputs.

This extreme case illustrates one of the dilemmas resulting
from escalation, in particular, and import-substitution policy oriented
toward final products, in general. Maintenance of low protection on
intermediate inputs, when the exchange rate is overvalued, is equivalent
to relative subsidization of imports of such products. The resulting
tendency of imports of intermediate goods to expand frustrates attempts
to extend import substitution to these categories. Moreover, the country's composition of imports becomes inflexible, increasing the danger
of a trade gap, since imports of inputs can not be compressed without
creating a bottleneck on industrial production throughout the economy.

Recourse to escalation by virtually all countries has the result
that composition of world trade contains a disproportionate share of
inputs and that finished products are subject to universal discrimination.
To the extent that these finished manufactures are labor intensive, this
has the result of frustrating the trade of those developing countries
which have a potential comparative advantage in such products.

RELATIVELY LOW DUTIES ON CAPITAL GOODS

A special case of escalation is the tendency to apply relatively
low tariffs, or no protection at all, to capital goods. This tendency
appears clearly in Charts 7 through 14, and again in Chart 17, in
which the average of 11 LAFTA countries' scheduled duties on SITC

TABLE 7

Argentina: Principles of Tariff Reform

Part I
General level of duties

		_1_	_2_	_3_	_4_	_5_	_6_	_7_	_8_	_9_	_10_
(I) Inputs	(1)	40	50	60	70	80	90	100	110	120	130
	(2)	5	5	10	20	20	20	30	30	40	40
(II) Consumer Goods	(1)	110	110	120	120	130	130	130	130	140	140
	(2)	30	40	50	60	70	80	90	100	110	120
(III) Capital Goods	(1)	40	50	60	70	70	80	80	90	90	100
	(2)	30	30	30	40	40	40	40	50	50	50

Degree of processing

Part II
Level of duties for agriculture

		_1_	_2_	_3_	_4_	_5_	_6_	_7_	_8_	_9_	_10_
(I) Inputs	(1)		20	50	60	80	110				
	(2)		10	20	20	30	40				
(II) Consumer Goods	(1)			50	70	110	120	140			
	(2)				60	80					
(III) Capital Goods	(1)	110	110	10							
	(2)	10	10	10							

Degree of processing

Source: Roberto T. Alemann, " La Reforma Arancelaria en la República Argentina," in Instituto para la Integración de América Latina, Hacia una Tarifa Externa Común en América Latina, p. 203.

71 (nonelectrical machinery) is almost as low as the average duties on raw materials or on basic metals. Since it is common to grant ad hoc exemptions from duties on imported capital goods, in connection with new investments, the real nominal levels of protection in this category are undoubtedly much lower than the averages of scheduled tariffs indicated on the charts.

Given the input-like aspect of capital goods and the general feeling that investment should be encouraged at any cost, it is easy to rationalize this policy, even though it tends to inhibit the extension of import substitution to indigenous capital-goods industries and to inflate the import component in total investment. Indeed, although the import coefficient of investment depends on several variables (including size of country), it is not only much higher in underdeveloped countries than in developed countries, but also much higher in today's developing countries than it was in the present developed countries when they were at a comparable stage of development.[34]

There are strong reasons for believing that such high import coefficients in investment are in good part a reflection of distorted relative prices, distorted at least relative to other importables. The question of relative prices of capital goods is a complex one, however, because in a situation of chronic inflation and repeated devaluation their price ratios are higher than is the case with those nontradables and wage-goods and services that dominate most of the domestic economy (see Table 3, Chapter 3). Also, the international terms of trade for acquiring machinery and similar goods are said to be relatively unfavorable from the standpoint of developing countries, in part because of the effect of tied aid. The answer to the question of whether the domestic policy reflected in relatively low tariffs on capital goods tends to correct other influences or whether it introduces new distortions into the savings and investment process is not easy to analyze empirically.[35]

On a priori grounds, one can guess that the systematic domestic underpricing (relative to other imports) of imported capital goods, particularly the very modern and sophisticated equipment that can be obtained only from North America or Europe, introduces a substantial bias toward use of the most capital-intensive techniques of production. Whether this is a good or bad thing is a matter of controversy. Albert O. Hirschman hypothesized that use of the most modern technology in large-scale, capital-intensive ventures will stimulate dynamic development, create badly needed management skills, and offset the lower labor productivity of developing countries.[36] If true, this is an argument for import substitution, since there is evidence that the most capital-intensive industries in Latin America have been precisely those import-substitution industries in which foreign capital has

brought in with it the most advance equipment and technology. [37]
There is also some evidence, at least for Brazil, that such industries
have had, as Hirschman predicted, the most far-reaching repercussions
on the domestic economy through linkage effects.[38] On the other hand,
Hirschman's suggested strategy seems to run counter to comparative
advantage, to raise the capital-output ratio, and thereby to limit the
labor-absorptive capacity of industry. The present tendency among
development economists appears to favor this latter point of view,
viz., that intermediate technologies are likely to be more appropriate
for developing or semi-industrialized countries than the most advanced
technologies. A recent ECLA study points out that

> the incentives to the use of capital in place of manpower
> which are provided by many of the policies or practices
> in force sharpen the trend towards inefficient utilization
> of capital that stems from unduly small scales of produc-
> tion and other circumstances whose impact is the same.
> In effect, not only does the price system seem to reveal,
> in significant respects, a bias in favor of the use of capi-
> tal, but in addition the increasingly frequent application
> of measures representing capital subsidies (tax exemp-
> tions, and credits for industry on privileged terms) exert
> pressure in the same direction. The consequences are
> deplorable not only for the employment situation, but
> also, and above all, for the growth of the product, on
> which the inappropriate allocation of the region's scanty
> supply of capital has a detrimental effect.[39]

DIFFERENTIATION OF PROTECTION ON CLOSELY RELATED PRODUCTS

A graphic example of the tendency of levels of nominal protection
(and also of effective protection) to be highly differentiated within
product categories in countries following extremely import-substitutive
commercial policies was given in Chart 2, "Profile of Nominal Tariffs:
Argentina, MFN, 1965," which showed wide dispersion (measured by
standard deviations) within SITC two-digit classifications. This dispersion was greatly reduced by the 1967 tariff reform, as shown in
Chart 3, but it was still relatively much greater than in the common
external tariff of the EEC (Chart 1).

This tendency toward intraclass dispersion of rates is mainly
the result of application throughout Latin America of the tariff principle
embodied in the Brazilian "Law of Similars." It can also be seen,
by comparing lines 1 and 2 in Table 7, how this principle was systematically built into the reformed Argentine tariff structure.

Another source of intraclass differentiation of tariff rates can
be found in the results of item-by-item tariff negotiations with foreign
countries within either the GATT or a strictly bilateral context. Indeed,
it is characteristic of this bargaining process that concessions are
usually given for very minutely defined products. This is probably by
now the main reason for seemingly illogical variations of tariff rates
in those industrial countries (for example, the United States) that have
participated in a number of GATT negotiations.

For similar reasons, the procedures of LAFTA trade-liberalization negotiations and of LAFTA complementarity agreements also
lead to minute differentiation of intra-LAFTA preferences.

Finally, there is probably a more or less random element in
the dispersion of rates of protection in countries like Chile, where
the protective structure has not undergone thorough revision for years
and where the historical process of cost-push inflation has been such
that specific pressure groups have obtained ad hoc relief at different
times.

The question may arise whether a highly differentiated tariff
structure is intrinsically harmful, and, if so, to whom.

During the Kennedy Round negotiations, it was claimed that the
greater dispersion of U.S. tariff rates as compared to those of the
EEC put the Community countries at a disadvantage unless special
rules were devised for lopping off the highest tariffs (écrêtement)
before proceeding with across-the-board linear reductions. A study
by Richard Cooper[40] indicated that, given the parameters (estimated
price elasticities, levels of trade, height of tariffs, etc.) involved in
that particular situation, the higher U.S. tariff dispersion would not
place the EEC at a disadvantage.

Cooper's analysis dealt only with national advantage as viewed
in the special context of international trade negotiations, in which
"contrary to standard analysis, the gain from reciprocal tariff reduction accrues from the expansion of exports, the expansion of imports
appearing as a necessary cost."[41] Here, however, we are more concerned with the effects on the Latin American countries' own economies, and not with the possible damage to the mercantilistic interests of their trading partners. Even without rigorous analysis it would
appear that the welfare loss from excessive dispersion of rates of protection on products using similar factors and input mixes might be
considerable, because, among other reasons, it strengthens monopoly
positions and inhibits firms from diversifying into related lines of
production.

NOTES

1. Hollis B. Chenery, "Patterns of Industrial Growth," American Economic Review L, 4 (September, 1960), 624-53.

2. Cf. Donald B. Keesing, "Outward Looking Policies and Economic Development," Economic Journal (June, 1967), pp. 303-05.

3. Gordon C. Winston, "Notes on the Concept of Import Substitution," Pakistan Development Review, VII (Spring, 1967), 107-17.

4. Alfred Maizels, Industrial Growth and World Trade (London: Cambridge University Press, 1963), pp. 148-49.

5. Chenery, op. cit., p. 628. For criticisms of Chenery's article, see Winston, op. cit., and M. D. Steuer and C. Voivodas, "Import Substitution and Chenery's Patterns of Industrial Growth - A Further Study, "Economia Internazionale XVIII, 1 (February, 1965), 47-77.

6. ILPES, La Brecha Comercial y la Integración Latinoamericana (Mexico: Siglo Ventiuno Editores S.A., 1967), pp. 48-75.

7. Celso Furtado, Formação Economica de América Latina (Rio de Janeiro: LIA, Editor S.A., 1969), p. 135.

8. Stephen R. Lewis, Jr., On a Measurable Model of "Successful" Import Substitution, Research Memorandum No. 7 (Williamstown, Mass.: Center for Development Economics, Williams College).

9. Bela Balassa and Associates, The Structure of Protection in Some Developing Countries (Baltimore: Johns Hopkins Press, 1971), Appendix to Chapter 1.

10. Abba Lerner, "The Symmetry between Export and Import Taxes," Economica, New Series (Vol. III, August, 1936), reprinted in Lerner, Essays in Economic Analysis (London: Macmillan, 1953), pp. 123-33.

11. R. I. McKinnon, "Intermediate Products, Differential Tariffs, and a Generalization of Lerner's Symmetry Theorem," Quarterly Journal of Economics, 80, 4 (November, 1966), 584-615.

12. Barend A. De Vries, Export Experiences of Developing Countries (Washington, D.C.: IBRD, 1967), Chapter 4.

13. Elvio Baldinelli, "Arancel externo, tipos de cambio y

estabilidad monetaria, '' in INTAL, Hacia una Tarifa Externa Común en América Latina (Buenos Aires: INTAL, 1969), p. 162.

14. Furtado, op. cit., pp. 145-59. See also David Felix, ''An Alternative View of the Monetarist-Structuralist Controversy,'' and Joseph Grunwald, ''The Structuralist School on Price Stabilization and Economic Development: The Chilean Case,'' in Albert O. Hirschman, ed., Latin American Issues: Essays and Comments (New York: Twentieth Century Fund, 1961), pp. 81-123.

15. The more recent of these studies is The Performance of Developing Countries as Exporters of Manufactures to the Developed Market-Economy Countries (TD/B/C.2/91, December 22, 1969).

16. Nathaniel H. Leff, ''The Exportable Surplus Approach to Foreign Trade in Underdeveloped Countries,'' Economic Development and Social Change, 17, 3 (April, 1969), 346. See also Leff, ''Export Stagnation and Autarkic Development in Brazil, 1947-1962,'' in Charles 'T. Nesbitt, ed., op. cit., pp. 219-34.

17. Cf. Albert O. Hirschman, ''The Political Economy of Import-Substitution Industrialization in Latin America,'' Quarterly Journal of Economics, 82, 1 (February, 1968), 27.

18. S. B. Linder, Trade and Trade Policy for Development (New York: Frederick A. Praeger, 1967).

19. UNCTAD, The International Division of Labor and Developing Countries (New Delhi Conference document TD/40, January 19, 1968), Bela Balassa, ''The Impact of the Industrial Countries' Tariff Structure on their Imports of Manufactures from Less-Developed Areas,'' Económica, XXXIV, 4 (November, 1967), 372-83.

20. Statement of Carlos Manuel Castillo, in Inter-American Development Bank, The Process of Industrialization in Latin America, Round Table (Guatemala, April, 1969), p. 254.

21. Albert Small, ''Trends in U. S. Manufactured Imports from the Primary-Commodity-Exporting Countries'' (unpublished draft).

22. (Free translation.) J. Márquez, ''Los aranceles Latinoamericanos y su efecto sobre la integración económica de la región,'' Banco Central de Venezuela, Revista de Economía Latinoamericana (June 21, 1966), 102-03.

23. UNCTAD, Incentives for Industrial Exports: Parts One and

Two, TD/B/C.2/89, November 27, 1969, and 89/Add. 2, 1, December 3, 1969.

24. Ibid, table on p. 3.

25. Gottfried Haberler, "Import Taxes and Export Subsidies: A Substitute for the Realignment of Exchange Rates," Kyklos, XX (1967), 23.

26. Balassa and Associates, op. cit., Chapter 4.

27. Montague Yudelman and Frederic Howard, Agricultural Development and Economic Integration in Latin America (Washington, D.C.: Inter-American Development Bank, April, 1969), pp. 143-49.

28. Theodore W. Schultz, "Economic Growth Theory and Profit in Latin American Farming," in Inter-American Development Bank, Agricultural Development in Latin America: The Next Decade, Round Table (Washington, D.C., April, 1967), pp. 169-88.

29. Harry G. Johnson, "Tariffs and Economic Development," op. cit., pp. 6-11. Johnson, incidentally, claims that only the optimum tariff argument (i.e., Scitovsky's terms-of-trade argument) provides an economic justification for tariffs, all other arguments for protection are arguments for subsidies" (p. 8).

30. For brief summary, see W. M. Corden, Recent Developments in the Theory of International Trade (Princeton, N.J.: International Finance Section, Princeton University, Special Papers in International Economics, No. 7, March, 1965), pp. 60-61.

31. Edmar Bacha and Lance Taylor, Foreign Exchange Shadow Prices in Chile: Conflicting Theories and Comparative Evaluations (Santiago: Oficina de Planificación Nacional, October, 1969), p. 21.

32. Ian Little, Tibor Scitovsky, and Maurice Scott, Industry and Trade in Some Developing Countries: A Comparative Study (London: Oxford University Press, 1970), p. 159.

33. Cf. Peter Eckstein, Toward an Integrated Theory of Tariffs, Discussion Paper No. 9 (Ann Arbor: University of Michigan Center for Research on Economic Development, August, 1969), pp. 29-35.

34. Nassau A. Adams, "Import Structure and Economic Growth: A Comparison of Cross-Section and Time-Series Data," Economic Development and Cultural Change (January, 1967), pp. 148-49.

35. See Carlos F. Díaz-Alejandro, Precios relativos y formación de capital en la República Argentina (Buenos Aires: Instituto Torcuato di Tella, Documento de Trabajo No. 29, 2a. edición, 1968), passim.

36. Albert O. Hirschman, The Strategy of Economic Development (New Haven, Conn., Yale University Press, 1958), pp. 143-55 (paperback edition).

37. Carlos F. Díaz-Alejandro, "Industrialization and Labor Productivity Differentials," Review of Economics and Statistics, XLVII, 2 (May, 1965), 207-14.

38. Werner Baer and Isaac Kerstenetzky, "Import Substitution and Industrialization in Brazil," American Economic Review, LIV, 3 (May, 1964), 411-25.

39. ECLA, The United Nations Second Development Decade: Industrial Development in Latin America (E/CN.12/830, March 13, 1969), p. 64.

40. Richard N. Cooper, "Tariff Dispersion and Trade Negotiations," Journal of Political Economy, LXXII, 6 (December, 1964), 597-603.

41. Harry G. Johnson, "An Economic Theory of Protectionism, Tariff Bargaining, and the Formation of Customs Unions," Journal of Political Economy, LXXII, 3 (June, 1965), 256-83. (Quoted from abstract.)

Economic integration differs from other forms of international cooperation in that, to the extent that it attains its goal of mutual trade liberalization and, ultimately, a common external tariff, it involves equalization of price levels on tradable goods within the area, except for those differences (reflecting mainly transport costs, product differentiation, internal indirect taxes, and trade markups) that are not related to protective measures. This would seem to be implicit in the definition of a common market.* It is therefore rather surprising that so little emphasis in the literature on Latin American integration has been on this fact, that sooner or later both the internal price levels of tradable goods and the ratios of various prices as compared with those in the outside world have to be brought into close alignment. Indeed, many measures taken in the name of integration often seem designed to perpetuate intra-area price divergence.[1]

CUSTOMS UNION THEORY

The theory of customs unions involves mainly the application of the principle of comparative advantage to a special case of systematic geographical discrimination in the protective system.[2] The analysis of gains from trade (or losses from protection) is more complicated than in ordinary comparative-cost theory, in which optimal free trade

---

*This is not the case, of course, in a free-trade area in which the retention of national external tariffs plus the application of complicated rules of origin prevent (in the case of goods having substantial content of dutiable inputs) the full harmonization of prices through intra-area arbitrage.

112

is the criterion. Both the point of departure of the process analyzed and its objective (e.g., customs union, free-trade area, etc.) are nonoptimal situations. Much of this body of theory is devoted to showing how little can be said a priori about the effects of integration in general. This follows from the "theory of second-best," which has been summarized as follows:

> If it is impossible to satisfy all the optimum conditions (in this case to make all relative prices equal to all rates of transformation in production), then a change which brings about the satisfaction of some of the optimum conditions (in this case making some relative prices equal to some rates of transformation in production) may make things better or worse.[3]

While this may not seem very helpful for our purposes, it at least clears away any facile assumption that integration is always a good thing.

Calculation of the static welfare results of integration is usually carried out in terms of Viner's distinction between trade-creation effects (when a change in protection induces a shift of trade from a high-cost source to a lower-cost source) and trade-diversion effects (when a higher-cost source replaces what had been a relatively low-cost source).[4] Viner was inclined to be pessimistic, on balance, about what the algebraic sum of these two effects would yield in real-life integration schemes. Subsequent authors have refined the subtlety of the theory without changing the general agnosticism as to whether integration is or is not likely to be advantageous and, if so, to whom.[5] What is remarkable is that very few have evaluated specific schemes in the light of empirically measured relative prices (i.e., measured protective systems), despite the fact that these are among the key variables on which the judgment depends.

As far as static gains and losses are concerned,[6] economic theory is particularly dubious about the net advantages of integration among developing countries. However, as Sidney Dell, Bela Balassa, and others have pointed out, such considerations based on the traditional theory of customs unions do not rank high among the reasons why developing countries, and Latin American countries in particular, are interested in integration.[7] As between development and integration, the former is always given priority, and the predominant arguments for integration cited by spokesmen of developing countries have to do with achieving economies of scale, pursuing import substitution at the regional level, reducing external vulnerability, and increasing bargaining power vis-à-vis the industrial countries.[8] It is nevertheless of interest to speculate on how Latin American integration would measure up to the Vinerian test.

EXTRAREGIONAL REPERCUSSIONS

First, the problem can be simplified somewhat by ignoring possible adverse effects on outside countries. This is not a matter of a double standard favoring developing countries, but merely recognition that the pattern of trade dependence is such that, while trade diversion resulting from commercial-policy measures in the United States can greatly affect Latin American terms of trade, there is relatively little damage that Latin American measures can do to the trade of industrial countries unless there is discrimination as among different industrial countries or groupings of industrial countries. This is apparent from Table 8. By and large, in the absence of such discrimination among outsiders, Latin America can consider its terms of trade as given by the world market as far as imports are concerned. As for nontraditional exports, implementation of general preferences for developing-country manufactures, or of special preferences for Latin American manufactures, would probably improve Latin American terms of trade with developed countries, but this would not affect or be affected by Latin American integration. Latin American countries are already manipulating--or trying to manipulate-- their terms of trade with respect to those traditional products, best exemplified by coffee, in which they have an oligopolistic position, and it is doubtful that further progress toward integration would change this situation very much, if at all.

Although the share of total North American exports taken by Latin America is relatively large (11 per cent), this does not mean that North America need fear significant trade damage from greater Latin American integration, whether this merely takes the form of regional-level import substitution replacing national-level import substitution or is accompanied by a greater opening-up of the Latin American economies and significantly increased two-way trade with the outside world. Individual U.S. exporting industries and import-competing industries will be affected differently, but adjustments to the changing composition of trade are constantly occurring in any event as an accompaniment to erratic changes in Latin American commercial policies and balance-of-payments vicissitudes. The net trade position of the United States toward Latin America will continue to be mainly a function of aid policy and the level of financial resources made available to cover the Latin American trade and payments' deficit toward the United States.

On the other hand, the high Latin American tariffs would provide much scope for trade diversion as between North American and European sources if geographically discriminatory arrangements were to be introduced. This could happen if, for example, individual

TABLE 8

Patterns of Trade of Latin America
With Major Partner Areas,
1968
(exports, fob)

Partner Areas	Exports of Partner Areas to Latin America, As Per Cent of Their Total Exports	Exports of Latin America to Partner Areas, As Per Cent of Total Latin American Exports
North America	11 per cent	37 per cent
EEC	3	19
EFTA	4	9
Japan	4	5
Total industrial areas	6	74
Developing areas (other than L.A.)	1	4
Australia, N.Z., South Africa	negl.	negl.
State-trading area	4	6
World (non-L.A.)	4	89
Latin America (Intratrade)	11	11

Source: GATT, International Trade 1968 (Geneva: GATT, 1969), Appendix Table G.

Latin American countries or a Latin American trade bloc were to
associate with the European Economic Community under the type of
mutual preference arrangements--involving reverse preferences--
that exist between the EEC and the Yaounde group of African countries
and between the EEC and a growing number of Mediterranean countries.
Such trade diversion, if allowed to occur, could be extremely damaging
to the U.S. trade position. There is little doubt that the EEC would
be in a favorable strategic position to use the bargaining power of its
structural import surplus vis-à-vis Argentina and certain other Latin
American countries to seek preferential treatment there if it so desired. For the time being, this does not appear to be an imminent
danger because of the prior claims of Africa and other countries already enjoying privileged commercial relationships, because the
Community has not yet been able to develop a coordinated position on
trade relations with Latin America, because of probable sharp reac-
tions in the GATT-UNCTAD context as well as from the United States,
and because of pressures from domestic agricultural interests in the
EEC. It is clear that any serious attempt by either the EEC or the
United States to extend a system of mutual preferences to Latin
America would have immediate political repercussions.

It thus seems justified to limit consideration of the static trade-
creation and trade-diversion effects of Latin American integration to
those affecting that area itself.

AGRICULTURE

If Latin American integration measures were fully applied to
the agricultural sector, there seems little doubt that the static welfare
effects would fall definitely on the side of trade creation. As Montague
Yudelman and Frederic Howard have pointed out in a comprehensive
study on behalf of the Inter-American Development Bank,[9] the Latin
American Free Trade Association (LAFTA) already competes on the
world market in a wide variety of tropical, semitropical, and temperate
products and is, by definition, and efficient producer. Moreover, it
is not expected that an increase in intra-LAFTA trade would divert
substantial amounts of traditional export products from markets outside the region. Expanded intraregional trade in such products would
have the further advantage of not entailing a significant foreign exchange cost, direct or indirect.

The fact that integration in the agricultural sector would have
almost entirely trade-creating welfare effects does not make it any
easier to accomplish; on the contrary, it makes it more difficult,
since the inefficient national producers who, under trade creation,
are displaced by more efficient producers in the integration area are

precisely those who are politically most vocal. This is illustrated by
the frustrations encountered by Argentina in trying to get wheat on the
LAFTA Common List. Indeed, it was mainly the problem of how to
handle agriculture that caused the postponement of the LAFTA timetable for free trade beyond the 1973 target date and kept the Common
List--originally considered to be LAFTA's most important instrument--
indefinitely suspended. The 1969 report of the executive secretary of
LAFTA was extremely pessimistic with respect to any progress toward integration in the agricultural sector under the usual LAFTA
trade liberalization procedures, given the disparity in the cost structures within the region, the lack of consistent policies at the national
level, and particularly the marginality of much of the production in
the region as compared with the efficiency of the major commercial
producers.[10] The only way of advancing toward greater intratrade
in agriculture in the short run that the executive secretary could
suggest was through continued use of the ad hoc bilateral marketing
agreements between state-trading agencies through which most trade
in agricultural staples already occurs. He emphasized, however,
that the prinicipal obstacle to this solution lay in the market distortions
resulting from concessional sales of agricultural products by the
United States under P.L. 480.

Agriculture presents an instructive case for practical application
of the theory of customs unions in the light of the relative-price-level
definition of protection used in the present study. Yudelman's analysis
makes clear that the crux of the problem of integration is the process
of alignment of initially divergent price levels, and this is well brought
out in his case study of wheat in LAFTA. Table 9 illustrates the
magnitude of the price disparities involved, which, incidentally, have
no relationship whatever to the price disparities implied in the tariff
schedules. (Indeed, Argentina has the highest tariff on wheat in the
whole area.) The parallel with the situation that arose in implementing
the EEC's common agricultural policy is apparent, but with the difference that the price disparities are much greater within LAFTA. Thus,
it is in those areas where, according to customs-union theory, the
advantages of integration would appear to be greatest, that the political,
social, and human difficulties are also greatest. Yudelman also
stressed the interrelationship between the problems of agricultural
integration and the question of industrial protectionism, reflected in
unfavorable terms of trade for agriculture (high costs of inputs vs.
relatively low output prices).[11]

Like the executive secretary of LAFTA, Yudelman threw up his
hands at the insuperable difficulties facing integration in the agricultural sector through either automatic or negotiated liberalization of
intra-LAFTA trade aimed at unifying the price levels of these products.
He advocated a system of regional preferences applicable only to

TABLE 9

Wheat Support Prices in LAFTA Countries

Country	Year	Support prices ($ per metric ton)	
Argentina	1966/67	55	
Bolivia	1967	100	
Brazil	1967	109	
Chile	1967	82	
Colombia	1967	130	
Ecuador	1968	108	
Mexico	1968	73	(Central and North)
		64	(Northwestern Pacific Zone)
Paraguay	(n.a. but estimated to be "high")		
Peru	1966	80	
Uruguay	1967	51	
Venezuela	(n.a.)	(n.a.)	

Source (except for Brazil): Yudelman and Howard, Agricultural Development and Economic Integration in Latin America (Washington, D.C.: Inter-American Development Bank, April, 1969); Brazil figure taken from Peter T. Knight, Brazilian Agricultural Technology and Trade: A Study of Five Commodities, (New York: Praeger, 1971), Table 19.

incremental demand or based on minimum regional quotas. An increase in intratrade of this nature, leaving the price disparities more or less untouched, may well be desirable, but it is not integration.

INDUSTRIAL SECTORS

Having discussed extraregional effects and agriculture, one can now ask what customs-union theory would be expected to tell us, a priori, about the internal resource-allocational effects of Latin

American integration in industry. For the time being, let us continue
to disregard the developmental goals of commercial policy (establishment of infant industries, creation of external economies and linkages,
discrimination against primary production in order to absorb redundant labor from the subsistence economy, adoption of policies to favor
depressed areas, etc.), which are considered much more important
in the scale of values of developing countries and of many development
economists than are the gains from trade dealt with in static customs-
union theory.

Viner's analysis led to the general proposition that "customs
unions are likely to cause losses when the countries involved are
complementary in the range of commodities that are protected by
tariffs," while benefits of trade creation will be greater if the respective economies are competitive, i.e., "the greater is the degree of
overlapping between the class of commodities produced under tariff
protection. . . ." This principle has been elaborated to show that the
gains from trade creation will be "larger the larger is the difference
between the opportunity costs at which the same commodity is produced
in the two countries."[12] But, as has already been brought out in
connection with agriculture, those commodities offering the greatest
scope for trade creation are also those where the political difficulties
of realigning relative price levels are greatest.

Other generally accepted propositions are that trade creation
will probably (but not necessarily) be greater the more countries
there are in the customs union, the larger the countries participating,
the higher the initial tariffs on competitive (overlapping) products,
the larger the preunion consumption of domestic commodities, the
smaller the proportion taken from the outside world, and the larger
the share of preunion foreign trade carried on with their future
partners.[13]

Putting these and other general propositions together and applying them to the LAFTA area, the only simple generalization that
can be derived is that of Balassa: "Given the high tariff levels in the
countries of Latin America, these propositions would indicate the
possibility of a considerable degree of trade creation and trade diversion in the area."[14] To go beyond this statement, it is clearly necessary to make an industry-by-industry, product-by-product analysis,
taking account of the protective measures actually applied to each
product and the effects on relative prices and costs, the patterns of
trade prior to and after integration, etc. The availability of such
information as would be found in internationally comparable profiles
of protection is thus of great importance for evaluating an integration
scheme; and the absence of such data in systematic form may be an
important reason for the dearth of empirically based evaluations of
Latin American integration groupings.

In addition to--and some would say in lieu of--the trade-creation/
trade-diversion analysis, it is important to consider not only the
developmental arguments for and against integration, but also and
particularly the technological question of economies of scale in relation to size of market. The gain in efficiency resulting from moving
from a national-size market to a regional-size market is in general
ignored by comparative-advantage theorists, or at least the analysis
is not well integrated into the theory of customs unions. This is ex-
plained by the fact that the assumptions of the pure theory of international trade usually exclude decreasing-cost industries, which are
difficult to handle in models based on perfect competition.[15] The
expansion of markets for such industries is understandably a dominant
preoccupation of the Latin American economists, since all Latin
American countries except Brazil, Argentina, and Mexico have total
national incomes in the range that would classify them as very small.
This explains the characteristic impatience with the comparative-
advantage or trade-creation/trade-diversion approach to integration
and the emphasis on the rationale of regional import substitution.[16]

Among the trade theorists, Bela Balassa[17] emphasizes both the
comparative-advantage and the market-size aspects of economic
integration. Under the latter heading he has stressed various kinds
of intraindustry economies of large-scale production (plant costs,
horizontal and vertical specialization) and also the so-called dynamic
external economies (growth of technological and organizational skill
and the development of linkages between industries).

Probably the only empirical research study that has yet attempted
to calculate the gains and losses from Latin American integration,
taking account not only of trade-creation/trade-diversion effects but
also of economies of scale (but leaving externalities out of consider-
ration), was conducted by the ECIEL group of 11 Latin American
research institutes under the coordination of the Brookings Institution.[18] This elaborate study used the analytical framework of location theory and linear programming techniques. Some of the specific
conclusions with respect to costs of production for various locations
of industry in LAFTA will be drawn on in the next chapter, but the
following statement on the relationship over time of scale effects to
trade-diversion effects is relevant to the present dicussion:

> This scale effect, yielding welfare benefits to consumers
> in the region, and the trade-diversion effect occur over a
> period of time rather than at a point in time. Thus, trade
> diversion to higher cost regional producers would not take
> place all at once, especially since trade among Latin
> American countries is currently quite small. Gradually,
> Latin American consumers would shift to Latin American

goods that, because of elimination of duties appear cheaper
to them. Habits and consumer responsiveness to price
differentials would vary the speed of the process from
country to country. At the same time, the growth of demand and the specialization of production would be lowering prices in these industries characterized by economies of scale. The gains from union would also be increasing over time as prices from optimum location plants
fell relative to national plants (assuming that output of
optimum location plants would be increasing relative to
national plants) and relative to third country imports net
of tariffs.[19]

THE LEAST-DEVELOPED-COUNTRIES PROBLEM

The most clear-cut type of economic loss through trade diversion
accompanying formation of an integration grouping is that likely to be
suffered by a small outward-oriented participating country, i.e., one
which had relatively low preunion tariffs on relatively large import
trade with countries outside the area. As customs discrimination in
favor of imports from its integration partners increases, and if this
is uncompensated by corresponding advantages for its exports within
the area, such a country's terms of trade may deteriorate sharply.
The situation will not be particularly serious in a free-trade area,
since the margin of trade-diverting preference given by the small
country on its intra-area imports will be limited by its own low
initial level of protection. In a customs union, on the other hand, the
margin of preference will ultimately rise as high as the new common
external tariff, unless special derogations are written into the integration arrangements for the benefit of the smaller partners. If the
import goods involved also have a high price elasticity, such as is
characteristic of many manufactured consumer products for which
the common tariff is likely to be very high, the loss through trade
diversion will be all the greater.

This small-country problem, which was exemplified in the EEC
by the efforts of the Benelux countries to keep the EEC common
external tariff as low as possible, becomes the least-developed-
country problem where the integration grouping is among developing
countries and where there are wide differences in the stages of development attained by the individual members. The least-developed
countries are likely to be particularly small (in terms of size of
domestic market), yet they are unlikely to reap significant benefits
of economies of scale and external economies from the integration
process since they do not have the type of industrial structure that is
subject to decreasing costs. Indeed, they may have very little

industrial structure at all. Moreover, their own exports--over-
whelmingly primary products--are oriented toward industrial countries
outside the integrating region and are unlikely to enjoy significantly
higher prices even if partly diverted toward their integration partners.
To be persuaded to join the grouping, therefore, they have to be bribed
by a combination of different kinds of special privileges, some of
which may directly alleviate these disadvantages and others of which
may provide real or imagined advantages in the domain of industrial
development.

     The issue has been exacerbated by the rapidly increasing polit-
ical self-consciousness of these least-developed among the developing
countries. The appearance of this special pressure group has been
one of the most important features of the development of UNCTAD
since the 1964 Geneva Conference. In the UNCTAD forum, the political issue arises from the fact that the preindustrial countries--mainly
in Africa--do not expect advantages from the scheme for generalized
preferential access to developed-country markets for manufactured
goods. Since these countries are numerous (and, therefore, powerful
under United Nations voting rules), they have placed a high price on
any "log-rolling" cooperation with the semi-industrialized countries
of Latin America and Asia which export--or (in the case of Latin
America) aspire to export--manufactured goods. Oratory on this
subject has been strident in UNCTAD meetings; the secretariat has
had to devote much research effort to such questions as the indenti-
fication of least-developed countries and the development of proposals
for special compensations drawn from the wide gamut of international
policy measures for which UNCTAD claims jurisdictional competence.[20]

     Among the policy areas in which the problem of special measures
for the least developed among the developing countries has been
studied and restudied by UNCTAD, ECLA, and other UN bodies, the
question of the division of gains and losses from economic integration
has probably received greatest attention. Emphasis has been placed
more on the possible frustration of the least-developed countries'
desire to carry out their own import-substitution policies, in order
to catch up with their more advanced partners, than on the trade-
diversion losses resulting from having to switch their imports from
a low-cost to a high-cost source. The measures proposed for ensuring
an equitable distribution of the benefits of integration tend to be
mainly of a protectionist nature--giving the least-developed countries
special derogations or delays from the general obligations for trade
liberalization within the grouping and establishing extra margins of
preference in their favor--or to call for ad hoc ("planned") decisions
for the location of new industries within their borders. Emphasis is
also placed on financial mechanisms for ensuring balanced trade and
for easing the intraregional payments deficits of the least-developed

countries, for compensating their revenue losses, for improving their
infrastructure through making available subsidized credits, etc.[21]
Such suggested remedies appear to be largely irrelevant. The real
hardship undergone by the least-developed countries under integration
does not lie so much in exposure to the competition of their partners
as in being cut off from the potential gains from trade with the world
market.

THE DEPRESSED-AREAS PROBLEM

Up to this point the terms "region" and "regional" have been
used to refer to geographic areas comprising more than one country,
as in speaking of the Latin American region or the Andean or River
Plate subregions. However, the new interdisciplinary field of regional science [22] deals mainly with what can be called subcountry regions
(e.g., the Northeast of Brazil), and it is with these that this section is
concerned.

There are many analogies between the least-developed-country
problem just discussed and the problems of disparities in economic
development or growth among areas that are parts of countries (or
parts of adjoining countries, like the Andean altiplano). Many development economists assert, for example, that international economic
integration such as that involved in formation of a free-trade area or
customs union will always tend to widen the gap between different
areas within countries.

An examination of the rationale and significance of these arguments would lead too far into the esoteric terminology of " spread"
effects" and "backwash effects,"[23] "trickling-down effects" and
"polarization effects,"[24] and Perroux-vian "growth poles," "development poles," and "integration poles."[25] In any case, the Latin
American integrationists are convinced that coordination of regional
investment policies within the integration framework can be so devised
as to counteract the centrifugal tendencies toward greater intracountry
regional disparities.[26]

Whether or not integration necessarily widens regional disparities
within countries, it is clear that all countries--large or small and
whatever their levels of development--are preoccupied with the
general problem. The United States has its Appalachia; France has
its Brittany; Italy has its Mezzogiorno; the United Kingdom has its
North; Brazil has its Northeast; etc. One suspects that too many
separate problems have been swept under the taxonomic heading of
"depressed areas." Nevertheless, however classified, they are
obviously very crucial political problems in Latin America, and it is

useful to inquire into their relationship to the structure of protection.

Chile offers a variety of discouraging examples of attempts to manipulate protection as an instrument of domestic regional policy. The Chilean protective regime involves all kinds of special treatment-- systematic or ad hoc--for favored industries, regions, and agencies. Various regimes involving _franquicias_ (exemptions from import duties, etc.) have been provided under a number of laws on behalf of the Departments of Arica, Iquique, Pisagua, Taltal, and Chañaral; the provinces of Chiloé, Aysén, Magallanes, Tarapacá, and Antofogasta; and in some cases, even particular communes are designated. Moreover, the president of the republic has the power to give drawbacks of up to 100 per cent of the tariffs on equipment for export industries, whenever a special locational criterion is met.[27] Aside from the fact that these arrangements make it extremely difficult for even the officials to know just what the nominal protection regime is in Chile (let alone evaluate the pattern of effective protection), it is doubtful that any real advantages obtained by the favored communes, departments, or provinces justify the numerous new problems created, including the incentive to smuggle from one area to another. Such commercial- policy measures taken in the name of regional development lured more than 20 automobile assembly plants--some of which produced only a handful of cars--to the unlikely location of Arica, 1,000 miles north of Santiago, where the principal market and the main suppliers of components were located. This did not improve the efficacy of import-substitution policies in the automotive industry.

Although it is questionable whether ad hoc customs concessions to designated depressed areas really help them very much, it seems quite probable that import-substitution policies, particularly those taken at the national level, have had the significant adverse effects of further depressing some of these areas and of frustrating the efforts made to correct the disparities by special transfusions of capital. This occurrence, which can be diagnosed through analysis of the structure of protection, occurs through regional differences in the terms of trade brought about by the protective system. By comparing relative prices and implicit exchange rates applicable to goods produced and consumed in East Pakistan and West Pakistan, Stephen Lewis has shown how, during the 1950's, primary production in the East wing was discriminated against relative to that in the West wing, while agriculture in both regions was kept at a disadvantage relative to the import-substitution industries.[28]

The best-known case of regional disparity in Latin America is that between the Northeast and the Center-South of Brazil. In 1966, per-capita income in the Northeast was one-third of that in the Center-South and only a little over a quarter of that in São Paulo

State.[29] In Brazil--as in Pakistan, Indonesia, the Congo, and Nigeria--
the periphery tends to be a net exchange earner, using its export
surplus toward foreign countries to buy industrial goods at protected
prices from the center. The 1959 report of the Brazilian Development
Council for the Northeast (the Furtado Report) analyzed the problem
as follows:

> By supplying foreign credits to the Center-South the
> Northeast has been contributing towards the development
> of the former, with a factor which is scarce for Southern-
> ers' capacity for importing. . . . As the Center-South
> exports to Northeast are made up chiefly of manufactured
> merchandise, whereas raw materials have much more
> weight in Northeastern exports, it is proper to surmise
> that the discrepancy favoring the Center-South is still
> greater, if the barter is measured in terms of the volume
> of employment created for both regions. . . . Foreign
> exchange proceeds which the Northeast did not spend for
> imports, but used for buying in the Center-South, suffered
> a drop in purchasing power of the magnitude indicated. . . .[30]

On the basis of the data from the Furtado Report and other information, it appears that the terms of trade of the Northeast vis-a-
vis the Center-South deteriorated from an index of 100 in 1948 to 48
in 1960, taking account of changes in the exchange rate. This perverse
transfer of resources through the interregional terms of trade largely
offset the flow of resources through the federal fiscal mechanism in
favor of the Northeast.

The problem of depressed areas obviously has many other
facets. Stefan Robock, a strong partisan of the import-substitution
strategy of development, has played down the role of the discriminatory
operation of the customs and exchange system as a significant factor
in the relative backwardness of the Brazilian Northeast.[31] However,
in view of the high nominal and effective protection on import-substitution goods and the negative protection on primary exports throughout
Latin America, there is every reason to expect that the plight of many
depressed areas has been greatly accentuated by the domestic terms-
of-trade disparity, which would appear to be comparable to that which,
according to the Prebisch thesis, characterizes the relationship
between developed and developing countries. Moreover, depending
on the eventual height of external tariffs, such interregional trade-gap
effects seem as likely to persist under import substitution at the
continental level as under national-level industial protectionism.

NOTES

1. For some highly theoretical discussion of various definitions of regional integration, see the following articles in Revista de la Integración (Buenos Aires: BID/INTAL, No. 5, November, 1969): Johan Galtung, "Una teoría estructural de la integración," pp. 11-49 Joseph S. Nye, "Integración regional comparada: concepto y medición," pp. 50-86; Enrique R. Melchior, "Fronteras internacionales y espacios económicos," pp. 191-202.

2. See Jaroslav Vanek, General Equilibrium of Inter-National Discrimination: The Case of Customs Unions (Cambridge, Mass: Harvard University Press, 1965), p. 1; R. G. Lipsey, "The Theory of Customs Unions: A General Survey," Economic Journal, 70 (1960), reprinted in Jagdish Bhagwati, ed., International Trade: Selected Readings (Harmondsworth, England: Penguin Books, 1969), p. 218.

3. R. G. Lipsey and K. G. Lancaster, "The General Theory of Second Best," Review of Economic Studies, 24, (1956-57), quoted in Lipsey, op. cit.,p. 220

4. Jacob Viner, The Customs Union Issue (New York: Carnegie Endowment for International Peace, 1950), Chapter 4.

5. Vanek, op. cit.,pp. 212-31, gives an impressive list of 107 general conclusions on the probable effects of customs unions and other forms of trade discrimination, covering various combinations of situations.

6. Cf. R. F. Mikesell, "The Theory of Common Markets as Applied to Regional Arrangements Among Developing Countries," in Roy Harrod and D. C. Hague, eds., International Trade Theory in a Developing World (London, 1963), p. 218; and Peter J. Lloyd, International Trade Problems of Small Nations (Durham, N.C.: Duke University Press, 1968), pp. 118-19.

7. Bela Balassa, Economic Development and Integration (Mexico: Centro de Estudios Monetarios Latinoamericanos, 1965), pp. 34-35; Sidney Dell, Trade Blocs and Common Markets (London: Constable and Co., 1963), pp. 160-65.

8. UNCTAD, Trade Expansion and Economic Integration Among Developing Countries (New York: United Nations, TD/B/85/Rev.1, Sales No. 67.II.D.20), pp. 6-10. See José-María Aragão, "La Teoría Económica y el Proceso de Integración de América Latina," Revista de la Integración (Buenos Aires: BID/INTAL, No. 2, May, 1968), passim.

9. Montague Yudelman and Frederic Howard, Agricultural Development and Economic Integration in Latin America (Washington, D.C.: Inter-American Development Bank, April, 1969), pp. 96-97.

10. ALALC, Apreciaciones sobre el Proceso de Integración de la ALALC (Montevideo: Asociación Latino Americana de Libre Comercio, 1969), pp. 55-67.

11. Yudelman and Howard, op. cit., pp. 98, 182-84.

12. R. Lipsey, op. cit., pp. 221-22.

13. Cf. Lipsey, ibid., p. 234; Lloyd, op. cit., pp.98, 118; Vanek op. cit., pp. 211-13. Antonio Calderón Martinez, De la ALALC al Mercado Común Latinoamericano, (Mexico: Colección ALALC de SELA, 1966), pp. 36-40.

14. Balassa, op. cit., p. 34.

15. ". . . The presence of economies of large scale production leads to multiple equilibrium and therefore introduces an intrinsic arbitrariness into the determination of the international patterns of specialization." John S. Chipman, "A Survey of Theory of International Trade: Part II, the Neo-classical Theory," Econometrica, XXXIII (October, 1965), 749, quoted in Lloyd, op. cit., p. 17.

16. See Calderón, op. cit., pp. 42-45; Victor L Urquidi, Teoria Realidad y Posibilidad de la ALALC en la Integracion Economica Latinoamericana: Dos Conferencias (Mexico: El Colegio de México, 1966), pp. 17-26.

17. Balassa, op. cit., Chapter and Appendix.

18. Martin Carnoy, ed., Industrialization in a Latin American Common Market (Washington, D.C.: The Brookings Institution, 1968), a study undertaken by Estudios Conjuntos de Institutos Economicos Latinoamericanos (ECIEL) and awaiting publication in book form. The main conclusions have been published in Martin Carnoy, "A Welfare Analysis of Latin American Economic Union: Six Industry Studies," in The Movement toward Latin American Unity, Ronald Hilton, ed., (New York: Frederick A. Praeger, 1969), pp. 237-71.

19. Carnoy, "A Welfare Analysis . . .", op. cit., pp. 246-47. See also G. Nguyen Tien Hung, "Economies of Scale and Economic Integration," Finance and Development, 5, 2, (June, 1968), 35-40.

20. See, for example, the following UNCTAD documents:
Special Measures to be Taken in Favor of the Least Developed Among
the Developing Countries Aimed at Expanding Their Trade and Im-
proving Their Economic and Social Development, New Delhi Conference
Resolution 24 (II) (TD/17, November 24, 1967, Special Measures in
Favour of the Least Developed Among the Developing Countries:
Identification of the Least Developed Among the Developing Countries
(TD/B/269, July 11, 1969); Report of the Group of Experts on Special
Measures in Favour of the Least Developed Among the Developing
Countries, held at the Palais des Nations, Geneva, from November 24
to December 5, 1969 (TD/B/288, December 18, 1969).

21. See UNCTAD, Trade Expansion and Economic Integration
Among Developing Countries op.cit., pp. 20-31.

22. For a brief survey, see J. Hilhorst, ''Regional Development
Theory: An Attempt to Synthesize,'' in Multidisciplinary Aspects of
Regional Development, Annual Meeting of Directors of Development
Training and Research Institutes, Montpellier, September 7-12, 1968.
(Paris: OECD Development Center, 1969).

23. Gunnar Myrdal, Economic Theory and Under-developed
Regions (London: G. Duckworth, 1957).

24. Albert O. Hirschman, The Strategy of Economic Development (New Haven, Conn.: Yale University Press, 1958).

25. Fransois Perroux, ''Multinational Investment and the
Analysis of Development and Integration Poles,'' in Inter-American
Development Bank, Multinational Investment . . .,op. cit., pp. 95-125.

26. See J. M. Aragão, '' Integración Latinoamericana y desarrollo nacional,'' Revista de la Integración, 42 (May, 1969), 152-80.

27. Oficiana de Coordinación del Supremo Gobierno con
el Sector Privado, Manual para Invertir en Chile (Santiago: Programa
de Asistencia Técnica Chile-California, 1967), II. D. 2.

28. Stephen R. Lewis, Jr., Economic Policy and Industrial
Growth in Pakistan (Cambridge, Mass.: MIT Press, 1969), pp. 94-97,
and Lewis, '' Effects of Trade Policy on Domestic Relative Prices:
Pakistan, 1951-64,'' American Economic Review, LVIII, 2 (March,
1968), 60-78.

29. Peter T. Knight, Brazilian Agricultural Technology and
Trade: A Study of Five Commodities (New York: Frederick A.
Praeger, 1971), Chapter 1.

30. Conselho de Descenvolvimento do Nordeste, A Policy for the Economic Development of the Northeast (1959), quoted by Werner Baer, "Regional Inequality and Economic Growth in Brazil," Economic Development and Cultural Change, XII, 3 (April, 1964), 278-79. See also, Stefan H. Robock, Brazil's Developing Northeast: A Study of Regional Planning and Foreign Aid (Washington, D.C.: The Brookings Institution, 1963), p. 108).

31. Ibid., pp. 58, 110-11.

CENTRAL AMERICAN COMMON MARKET

The five countries belonging to the CACM are all microstates, in terms of both population and national product, and the grouping as a whole is comparable in size to a small country--intermediate, say, between Peru and Columbia. However, as the first Latin American integration scheme to be implemented institutionally and to move to a common external tariff, its experience has attracted much attention.

Many of the political issues likely to appear in a broader common market have already arisen in the subregion, notably in the context of allocation of industries. Because of wide disparities in levels of development within the grouping, from Costa Rica and El Salvador at one extreme to Honduras at the other, the industrial policy of the CACM has been dominated by the least-developed-country problem. In the Central American context, this is primarily the Honduran problem, although Nicaragua has also raised claims for special treatment.* In August, 1970, Honduras announced its withdrawal from the CACM because of alleged insufficiency of the special arrangements in its favor. This decision was apparently reversed a month later, following the announcement that a new Fund to Finance Industrial and Agricultural Production was to be created under the financial sponsorship of the Inter-American Development Bank.

----

*An UNCTAD study (TD/B/269 of July 11, 1969) gives the following rankings according to a "composite index of development" in a list of 90 developing countries: Costa Rica, 20; El Salvador, 30; Nicaragua, 35; Guatemala, 38; and Honduras, 43.

The Central American Common Market was established under the intellectual guidance of the Economic Commission for Latin America (ECLA), and its commerical policy was dominated from the outset by ECLA's emphasis on import substitution, at the supranational level, as a development strategy. Although the initial customs duties in the member countries were mainly fiscal and relatively low by Latin American standards, as is characteristic of small outward-oriented exporters of primary products, the rates of the common tariff were set closer to the higher than to the lower range of the national rates. Subsequent developments led to further increases to protect particular industries. The common tariff's structure[1] is sharply escalated (tariffs on raw materials and capital goods having been lowered from the national tariff levels) and therefore yields very high levels of effective protection, notably in such categories as beverages, wood manufactures, shoes and clothing, food preparations, soap and detergents, and perfumes and cosmetics. On the other hand, resource-oriented and traditional-export activities--such as fishing, forestry, metallic mining, and agriculture--are discouraged by the negative effective protection resulting from export taxes and the positive nominal protection on inputs. There is also considerable differentiation within categories, depending on the existence of local production and on special exemptions from duties on inputs. As usual, the highest rates apply to consumer goods produced within the area.* Under the San José Protocol of June 1, 1968, a "temporary" surcharge was imposed on tariffs on imports from third countries.

What was intended to be the basic mechanism of industrial policy in the CACM was established by the Agreement on the System of Central American Integration Industries, signed in 1958 at Tegucigalpa, Honduras, as a companion document to the Multilateral Treaty on Central American Free Trade and Economic Development.[2] (This instrument set up the free-trade area which preceded the common-market stage subsequently established by the Treaty of Managua of 1960.) When it devised this scheme of integration industries, ECLA stressed both the need to achieve efficient utilization of the limited resources of Central America through economies of scale and the need to avoid duplication of investments or the appearance of excess capacity. Firms enjoying

---

*After this section was written, the author came across an excellent, but apparently unpublished, analysis, "Protection in the Central American Common Market in 1966," prepared under contract for USAID/ROCAP by Roger Lawrence of Columbia University, and containing, not only a wealth of empirical measurements of nominal and effective protection in the CACM, but also interesting methodological contributions and policy conclusions.

the special privileges of integration industries would be established,
one at a time, with due regard for the market capacity of the subregion.
In effect, this meant that each firm should have a monopoly. At the
same time, there was also the criterion of balanced development, i.e.,
such plants were to be evenly allocated among the five countries.
Indeed, a "transitional" article in the agreement provided that no
country should be allocated a second integration-industry plant until
each of the other members had received at least one plant. It will be
noted that considerations of intra-area comparative advantage or of
competitiveness with the outside world appear nowhere among the
criteria.

The monopoly privilege of an integration firm arises from the
fact that it enjoys free trade within all the member countries that
approved its establishment, while competitive products of an undesignated firm are subject to duties (decreasing 10 per cent a year for
ten years) in member countries other than the country in which the
undesignated firm is located. Also, an integration plant is exempted
from tariffs on its inputs for ten years, and it may be given other
special benefits. In return for these monopoly advantages, the plant
is subject to special obligations with respect to minimum Central
American equity ownership, minimum initial plant capacity, price and
quantity controls, and nondiscriminatory channels of distribution.
Because of the red tape involved in getting designated under such
conditions, and perhaps also because of the opposition of the U.S.
Agency for International Development and the international financial
institutions to the monopolistic feature, little recourse has in fact
been taken to the integration-industries procedure. The first plant to
function under this program was the GINSA tire firm, the Guatemalan
subsidiary of the General Tire and Rubber Company.[3] After applying
for integration status in 1962, it finally received duty-free treatment
in three countries outside Guatemala in 1965. A long controversy
ensued over whether and where a second tire plant might be designated
to limit GINSA's monopoly; Firestone finally entered into competition
with GINSA on the basis of Costa Rican investment-encouragement
measures taken at the national level, without waiting to be designated
an integration industry. Meanwhile, a caustic soda and chlorinated
insecticide plant (a subsidiary of the Hercules Powder Company) was
designated as an integration industry in Nicaragua, and a plate glass
factory was approved for Honduras. Honduras, however, has still not
approved the protocols on the integration status of the tire, soda, and
insecticide plants, and continues to levy duties on their products at
its border. Available information is still insufficient to evaluate
whether the first experiment has been sufficiently successful, in terms
of achieving lower costs as a result of larger-scale production, to
justify the monopolistic feature of the arrangement.

As an alternative to the regime for integration industries, which tries to deal out new plants on a one-for-each-country principle, El Salvador managed to obtain approval, in 1963, of a different approach-- the Special System for the Promotion of Productive Activities.[4] Firms obtaining this status from the CACM Executive Council are not legal monopolies, but, upon meeting certain conditions as to capacity and effective production of goods not currently manufactured in the area, they are given unusually high tariff protection, subject to the safeguard that such specially protective rates can be withdrawn in the event abusively high prices are charged. The system became effective when a Philips subsidiary in El Salvador began the production of light bulbs, and since then several other projects have come in under the scheme. It is generally considered more flexible than the integration-industry procedure, since it involves less regulation and decisions are subject to less political influence. On the other hand, it appears to ignore the criterion of "balanced development."

Finally, one should mention the influence of the special customs exemptions and other fiscal advantages given by CACM member countries at the national level as incentives for new investments. In an effort to avoid competition among the countries, to their mutual disadvantage, a Convention on Fiscal Incentives was signed in 1962. Honduras, however, insists that as a least-developed country it should be entitled to give greater incentives than the others, and its failure to ratify the convention has left the whole question of fiscal incentives in the domain of national policy.

As a net result of these systems for coordination of investment in the CACM, actual investment decisions appear to be more politically based than ever. The pattern of protection is becoming as differentiated as in other import-substitution-oriented areas of Latin America. The consequences thus far may not have been particularly harmful, and the countries themselves undoubtedly greatly prefer industrialization on the basis of import substitution to no industrialization at all. After all, "the building of the Common Market is an exercise in politics, and it is an exercise of the most delicate kind, involving as it does the ultimate question of national sovereignty."[5] Provided that the acronymic institutional superstructure of the CACM does not break down of its own weight (or under the tensions of a "soccer war"), it may be that this political exercise of balancing national interests in a bargaining process is, in itself, worth considerable sacrifice of abstract economic rationality. One may still regret, however, that "integrated" Central America appears to be following the lead of the pathologically protectionist countries farther south by allowing its price structure to become more distorted, with predictable consequences for agriculture, export trade, and monetary stability. *

LATIN AMERICAN FREE TRADE ASSOCIATION

Two principal approaches to integration are being followed under the Treaty of Montevideo and subsequent LAFTA instruments: the trade-liberalization program (i.e., the item-by-item negotiation of intra-area concessions for inclusion in the national lists, the common list, and the special lists of concessions in favor of relatively less advanced countries) and the complementarity agreements (which are the outcome of industry-by-industry negotiations).

During the first few years of LAFTA, the trade-liberalization approach gave statistically impressive results, at least as far as numbers of minutely subdivided items were concerned, but it soon became apparent that most of this progress was illusory. It was easy to liberalize items only as long as these did not bring competition to domestic industries. The momentum of the trade-liberalization process rapidly subsided, once it became a question of giving concessions involving more than the "water" in the tariffs. The failure to implement the first 25 per cent tranche of the common list, or even to complete negotiation of a second tranche, made it clear to all that the trade-liberalization approach had run out of steam. Indeed, the 1969 year-end LAFTA conference at Caracas had to amend the Montevideo Treaty so as to extend the trade-liberalization deadline from 1973 to 1980. Proposals for a more automatic (across-the-board or linear) procedure for eliminating restrictions on intratrade have been opposed by representatives of the major countries, notably Argentina and Brazil, with the result that those countries that desire--or claim they desire--dynamic new steps toward integration are pursuing this goal

---

*Among other problems of economic integration with which CACM has apparently had to cope--according to one political scientist-- are "spill-over effects" (desbordamientos), "fall-out" (radiación), "spill-backs" (regesiones), "brinkmanship" (amenaza de llevar al borde del abismo), the "self-encapsulation syndrome" (auto-enquista- miento), and "spill-around symptoms" (despárramo, i.e., a mixture of spill-over and self-encapsulation)--all this together with "zero- sum games" between governmental agencies and pressure groups over matters of location of industry, trade policy, coordination of agricultural policy, and tax harmonization. (For clarification, see Philippe C. Schmitter, "La dinámica de contradicciones y la conducción de crisis en la integración centroamericana," Revista de la Integración, No. 5 [November,1969], 87-151.)

through the subregional Andean Group.*

The other strategy advocated for getting LAFTA off dead-center aims at sectoral common markets, using the mechanism of the complementarity agreements.[6] These were provided for, in broad terms, by the original Montevideo Treaty of 1960, Article 16 of which provided that the contracting parties--

> 1. Shall endeavor to promote progressively closer coordination of their corresponding industrialization policies, and shall sponsor for this purpose agreements among representatives of the economic sectors concerned; and
> 2. May negotiate mutual agreements on complementary economies by industrial sectors.

The original regime for complimentarity agreements, governed by LAFTA Resolutions 15(I) and 48(II), provided that concessions for products imported under this system would be included in the national lists, and would therefore apply without discrimination to all member countries and not just to the countries that had negotiated them. Only two agreements were concluded under this arrangement during the first five years: the IBM-sponsored agreement of 1962 on statistical machines and the RCA/Philips-sponsored agreement of 1965 on electronic tubes. It was felt that extending the advantages of each arrangement over the entire LAFTA area was a factor inhibiting recourse to the complementarity procedure. Therefore--and despite earlier assurances given to GATT--Resolution 99 (IV), adopted at the end of 1964, removed the provision calling for most-favored-nation treatment of all members of LAFTA as far as complementarity agreements were concerned, although relatively less-developed countries continued to be eligible for benefits on an unconditional basis.

The new policy stimulated some 30 new proposals from the private sector in 1965. Only two of these--both between Brazil and

---

*The author regrets that, owing to lack of time and reliable documentation, it was not possible to include an analysis of the implications of the Cartagena Agreement, signed May 26, 1969, by Bolivia, Colombia, Chile, Ecuador, and Peru. (For text, see ALALC, Síntesis mensual, 49 [July, 1969], 283-316.) Although this is perhaps the most interesting development in Latin American integration to date, recent political developments in the Andean area make any speculation as to its further evolution very premature.

Uruguay--were approved by the governments, however. Another wave of proposals came in 1967, out of which there materialized a fifth agreement covering a relatively large number of chemical products and which applied to all the participating countries. Another important agreement--on petrochemicals--was signed by Bolivia, Chile, Colombia, and Peru in July, 1968, and was of special significance for several reasons. It marked the first use of the complementarity-agreement procedure as an instrument of the subregional (Andean Group) approach to integration. It provided for an automatic and irrevocable timetable of liberalization and for common external tariff rates systematically escalated according to levels of processing. It also contained a complete program for coordination of production policies and allocation of plants among the participants. The provisions for mutual reservation of markets and regulation of competition have, to be sure, caused the raising of some eyebrows.

A seventh agreement, signed in August, 1968, between Argentina and Uruguay and covering certain household goods, was of the more usual type, the concessions being revocable and applying within a limited part of LAFTA. The eighth agreement, signed in March, 1969, between Argentina and Mexico, covering a few glass products, was followed by a ninth agreement in October, 1969, between Brazil and Mexico, on electrical generators and transmission and distribution equipment. The tenth and 11th complementarity agreements, on office machines, were signed in June, 1970, by Argentina, Brazil, and Mexico. As of the end of 1970, a dozen other draft agreements, involving various combinations of countries, were at the negotiation or prenegotiation stage.

The philosophy of economic integration and industrial planning embodied in the system of complementarity agreements is inspired mainly by the desire to utilize economies of scale and to avoid excess capacity. Whereas the regime of integration industries in the CACM can be characterized as one of institutionalized monopoly, the complementarity agreements in LAFTA have more in common with government-supported cartel agreements. They do not appear to create any new competition and, if anything, they restrain competition. Conceivably, the economies of scale and specialization might eventually lower unit costs enough to result in exports of components or final products outside the countries participating in the agreements, or even to the world market; but there is no incentive that would seem to operate in that direction. A Brookings Institution study commented:

> Complementarity arrangements...can cause costly deviations from optimum resource allocation. For example, a certain item may be produced in two or more countries when only one country has a clear advantage in producing

and distributing it. To avoid unemployment in the high-
cost countries, complementarity agreements might be
entered into which would permit the high-cost producers
to remain in existence. Each country would specialize in
the production of a different part of the item.

While such specialization may be better than no
specialization at all, it still does not constitute an optimum allocation of resources. Thus, complementarity
agreements can freeze a trade pattern which could represent high social costs to the integration area.[7]

The type of specialization involved in the complementarity
arrangements superficially resembles the intraindustry specialization
which has been such a significant feature of trade liberalization among
the industrial countries, with the difference that in the Common Market
and EFTA this phenomenon occurred more or less spontaneously as an
accompaniment of across-the-board reduction of trade barriers, while
in LAFTA it is occurring under a governmental aegis, although based
on proposals initiated by the private sector. It is recalled that the
prevalence of intraindustry specialization in Europe has been attributed
to the operation of imperfect competition and is considered to be a
factor that cushions the competitive effects of trade liberalization.

The tariff concessions made under the complementarity regime
are so selective and so closely defined at the item level that they are
likely to increase rather than decrease the variability of the tariff
profile within sectors employing similar factor inputs. If the differentiation of a tariff structure is a more important criterion of its protectiveness than is its height, selective tariff reductions of this sort may
well augment the distortions of resource allocation. Whether this
effect is important enough to counterbalance the advantages achieved
through scale economies and market interpenetration is a question to
which there is probably no general answer.

Attempts have been made to extend the complementarity approach
from the intrasectoral to the sectoral level by more comprehensive
programming of the overall industrial development of the LAFTA
region. This policy, enunciated in Resolution 100 (IV) of December 8,
1964, on the "Program of Economic Integration and Complementary
Economies," provided inter alia as follows:

6. The establishment of equitable conditions of competition among the products of the region will stimulate
the gradual industrial reorganization of the area.

7. In order to achieve an equitable distribution of

the benefits of integration and because of the different
structures and levels of development of the countries of
LAFTA, it is necessary that the location of industries be
undertaken jointly and by plan.

8. In order to speed up the economic growth of the
countries classed as relatively less economically developed and of those mentioned by Resolution 71 (III) of the
Conference, the search for and assignment of concrete
industrial projects of a regional nature for those countries should be encouraged.

9. The planned locating of industries of a regional
nature in specified countries implies the adoption of a
common policy in the production sector under consideration.

10. The locating of industries of a regional nature
must be based on criteria of profitability and/or productivity, considering also the necessity for all the contracting parties, because of their participation in these
industries to obtain equitable benefits from the integration.

11. To the extent that technical and economic
conditions permit, participation of the greatest possible number of countries should be sought in the production of sectors developed or to be developed
regionally.[8]

. . . .

These criteria, if literally applied, would leave very little room
for considerations of comparative advantage or, for that matter, of
absolute advantage. In any case, implementation of the program has
not passed the study stage.

The policy is in the hands of the Advisory Committee on Industrial Development (CADI), which has study groups for four "basic"
industries (steel, pulp and paper, petrochemicals, and other chemicals).
Voluminous reports were issued on these industries by the secretariat
during 1969,[9] but the CADI has not met recently to consider them. In
any case, the recommendations in the reports were hardly bold as concerned promotion of greater competition within the region. The steel
study, for example, recommended mainly agreements for temporary
quotas to cover occasional trade in national surpluses of certain products. It explicitly rejected any notion of trade liberalization or application of comparative advantage in the steel sector, since such

measures "might prejudice plants now in operation and prevent implementation of projects considered to be of great importance within the
jurisdiction of each country." It left unchallenged the declaration of
the ILAFA (the Latin American steel industry association) that "It is
impossible to renounce the aspiration of Latin American countries to
decide for themselves their levels of self-sufficiency in steel, since
this is considered a basic activity for the development of the national
economies." When the Steel Study Group--composed of national repre-
sentatives--reviewed the secretariat's document, it went even further
in opposing real trade liberalization, let alone rationalization of the
industry at the regional level. Although the Steel Study Group called
for guaranteed and effective intrazonal margins of preference, it also
said that it would be impossible in most cases to negotiate reductions
of either low or high rates of customs duties. It therefore advocated
using nontariff and administrative measures as the main elements for
negotiation. Any tariff reductions would be held within quota limits
in order to defend domestic producers and guide them in their annual
planning. The advance draft protocol for a complementarity agreement
drawn up in accordance with these principles obviously contributes
nothing to harmonization of regional price and cost relationships and
very little to the creation of the economies of scale cited as the rationale for Latin American integration.

The executive secretary of LAFTA, in his report of April, 1969,[10]
complained particularly about the disorderly growth of the automobile
industry, with its excessive number of assembly plants and proliferation of fabricators of parts. He pointed out that the bilateral arrangements worked out in this sector between pairs of countries had been
valiant experiments, but accomplished little. Meanwhile, each member
country was continuing to install new automobile factories, forcing the
main producers to diversify their activities in the region, with predictable adverse effects on costs of production.[11]

The LAFTA executive secretary also mentioned textiles as
another entire industrial sector where selective negotiations under
LAFTA procedures have accomplished nothing.

All in all, the record of industrial-location policy within LAFTA
makes depressing reading and gives scant encouragement for the near
future. There is little if any suggestion in LAFTA documents that one
of the aims of industrial policy might be to bring absolute and relative
prices in the area closer to those in the world market so as to reduce
the economic cost of import substitution and perhaps make possible
new lines of industrial exporting to third countries. Such ideas are
nevertheless increasingly prevalent among influential Latin American
economists, even though not yet reflected in official integration policy.
This new, more liberal tendency is illustrated, for example, by Aldo

Ferrer's advocacy of an "integrated and open industrial system"
that would be oriented toward exports of manufactured products and
insertion of the system into the world economy.[12] Similarly, a recent
ECLA document on industrial development states:

> First of all, the central objective of this strategy should
> be to bring about substantial improvements in the ability
> to compete of Latin American industry so that it can ful-
> fil its role as the motive force of overall economic
> development. In other words, a profound change must be
> sought in the direction of the industrialization process
> so that industry may have larger markets, make the
> best possible use of its comparative advantage and
> technological progress and maintain an increasing
> flow of trade both with the other associated developing
> countries and with the developed countries.
>
> Hence, systems of industrial integration and the
> promotion of exports to world markets are two aspects
> of but one strategy.[13]

The new type of sectoral complementarity arrangement advocated by
this and other recent ECLA documents presupposes, perhaps over-
optimistically, that during the 1970's some method of automatic across-
the-board trade liberalization will be in operation within LAFTA and
that gradual tariff harmonization toward a common external tariff
will be in its initial stages. In such a context, broad agreements
covering whole sectors could accelerate the trade liberalization for
the goods concerned beyond the overall rate of liberalization. Besides
the tariff provisions, the agreements would include indicative regional
development programs (as distinguished from rigid planning and
division of markets), an appropriate program of investment and technical assistance, and provision to harmonize fiscal incentives and regimes
on social security, foreign capital, etc.[14]

The less-developed countires of LAFTA are Paraguay, Ecuador,
and Bolivia. Uruguay received such status on a temporary basis in
1967, despite the fact that it has had one of the highest standards of
living in the area.* LAFTA rules also take special cognizance, for

---

*The UNCTAD Secretariat (TD/B/269 of July 11, 1969) ranks
the LAFTA countries (among the 90 developing countries considered)
as follows: Argentina, 2; Uruguay, 8; Chile, 9; Mexico, 10; Peru, 19;
Colombia, 23; Brazil, 25; Paraguay, 27; Ecuador, 28; and Bolivia, 44.
Venezuela was not classified because of data difficulties.

some purposes, of the problems of those countries which are not in
the less-developed category but which are "of insufficient market
size" (i.e., Chile, Colombia, Peru, Uruguay, and Venezuela).

Although there has been about 100 per cent increase in trade
flows from the less-developed and the other members of LAFTA
between 1962 and 1965 (the last year for which detailed data on a
comparable basis are available), analysis of the statistics indicates
that special concessional arrangements in favor of the former did not
play a very significant role in this expansion, most of which was
accounted for in the Paraguay-Argentina relationship and in items on
which there were no special concessions.[15]

COMPARISONS OF COSTS OF PRODUCTION
WITHIN LAFTA

Judging by the LAFTA policies with respect to industrial complementarity, as described in the preceding section, it would appear
that relative cost of production is only an academic--if not irrelevant--
consideration. Nevertheless, several interesting efforts have been
made to measure empirically the divergence of the cost profiles of
key industries as among the different member countries, despite the
methodological difficulties inherent in this kind of cross-country
comparison.

In 1967, the Argentine research institute FIEL (Fundación
de Investigaciones Económicas Latinoamericanas) conducted a very
ambitious study of this nature on the structure of industrial costs in
LAFTA for the Unión Industrial Argentina. The study produced an
impressive stack of documents, but neither the detailed data nor the
conclusions have been made public (possibly because they indicated a
degree of relative competitiveness on the part of Argentine industry--
and therefore redundancy of Argentine protection--that could have
been embarrassing to the sponsoring industrial association). Estimates
were made of historic costs, costs at capacity production, and of the
costs of hypothetical plants in order to determine possible economies
of scale. Costs were broken down under such headings as labor, taxes,
duties, transport, etc. International comparability was ensured by the
fact that the same team of Argentine researchers collected the information in each of the eight countries covered (Argentina, Brazil, Chile,
Colombia, Mexico, Peru, Venezuela, and Uruguay). This study reportedly indicated that the main causes explaining the differences in cost
levels within LAFTA are insufficient utilization of economies of scale,
a high percentage of unutilized installed capacity, relatively high levels
of protection on inputs, as well as miscellaneous causes such as different factor and resource endowments of the countries.[16]

The World Bank has published several monographs containing
price and cost comparisons for individual product categories. In a
study of heavy electrical equipment, the cost profiles for the production
of such items as large transformers, generators, capacitors, etc., in
Argentina, Brazil, and Mexico were compared with those prevailing
in India, Pakistan, Spain, and industrialized countries.[17] The purpose
was primarily to evaluate the respective countries' competitiveness
vis-à-vis the international market, taking account of economies of
scale, structure of protection, and labor productivity. Effective protection, domestic resource cost per unit of foreign exchange saved,
and similar analytical concepts were utilized in the study. The price
disadvantage in the sector was estimated at 25-30 per cent in Brazil
and 40-45 per cent in Argentina and Mexico. However, widely differing
results were obtained for the separate products, showing how risky it
is to generalize about a country's competitiveness. The study concluded
that economic production of heavy electrical equipment might nevertheless be possible within LAFTA, provided that the number of protected
producers was reduced, that there was more orderly procurement by
power companies, and that such equipment was subject to free trade
in the area with only moderate protection vis-à-vis third countries.

The World Bank's study on the automotive industries[18] compared production costs for a small car, a large car, and a light truck
made by the same international firm in Argentina, Brazil, Mexico,
and the United States. It was found that ex-factory costs of light truck
manufacture were 2.5 times U.S. costs in Argentina, 1.7 times in
Brazil, and 1.6 times in Mexico, and that the ratios of domestic
resource costs per dollar of foreign exchange saved were, respectively,
1.85, 1.17, and 1.92 (or 1.92, 1.28, and 1.65 net of estimated indirect
taxes). Brazil's advantage over Argentina was mainly attributable to
the size of its domestic market, to the proliferation of models and
parts in the latter country, as well as to differences in the tariff and
exchange-rate structures.

> The major element contributing to the high cost of
> vehicle manufacture in Latin America is local procure-
> ment of materials and parts, which are either protected
> or carry high import duties. In Argentina, material
> and parts average 3.3 times U.S. cost levels, and they
> constitute about 75 per cent of total costs.[19]

The Baranson study also contained a brief review of the frustrating
history of efforts to rationalize the location of the automobile industry
and to achieve specialization and scale economies within LAFTA. It
found that the bilateral complementarity arrangements negotiated
since 1965 among Argentina, Brazil, and Mexico (and which are outside
the regular LAFTA complementarity arrangements) have been very

limited in nature and have actually raised production costs. Although the individual countries do have complementarity advantages in specific components, national policies have inhibited exploration of these intra-industry specialization possibilities. According to Baranson, the LAFTA automotive market, although expected to grow to about 1,125,000 vehicles by 1975, could economically support no more than five major manufacturing complexes in the region, each producing basic types of vehicles. At present, average runs are only about 10,000 units a year as compared with the accepted optimum scale of 240,000 units.

An attempt to measure the economies of scale obtainable from integration of the steel industry within LAFTA, and to identify the most economic countries of location from the scale-economy standpoint was made by Argentine economist Martirena Mantel.[20] She used a computerized linear-programming model. The solutions obtained illustrate the interaction of three factors: transport costs, market size, and total cost per unit produced. Transport costs limit the influence of market size and of low unit costs. Therefore, it would not be economic to concentrate the entire production of the area in Colombia, the lowest-cost producer. Moreover, Argentina, Brazil, and Mexico already have relatively large internal markets giving substantial economies of scale within their own frontiers, so, as far as these countries are concerned, regional integration would have little advantage over autarky. However, the autarkic solution, in which all countries in the area made their own steel, would involve a 12 per cent higher cost than the optimal solution generated by the model, in which the area would be supplied from Colombia and Chile. It should be borne in mind that this is a purely illustrative model, mainly of methodological interest as an application of linear-programming techniques. The empirical data on which the solutions are based were drawn from an ECLA study of the Latin American steel industry in 1954 and presumably have little relationship to present-day reality.

A much more elaborate application of this general approach is to be found in the Brookings/ECIEL project on industrialization in a Latin American common market.[21] The participating research institutions agreed upon a list of 14 products from six industries that covered a wide range of the manufacturing sector. The industries studied were fertilizers, methanol-formaldehyde, paper and pulp, powdered milk and cheese, tractors, and universal parallel lathes. The demand of the individual countries for these products was projected and summed to give total LAFTA demand in 1975. Taking account of existing installed capacity and of plans for expansion already in course of implementation, the problem posed was to estimate the level and structure of the costs and to determine the optimal locations of the plants that would have to be established in order to satisfy the demand of the LAFTA area projected for 1975 under the assumption of a complete absence of trade barriers. Although the study concentrated on possible economies-of-scale effects of integration among the LAFTA countries, the welfare estimates derived therefrom included also the gains and losses from trade creation or diversion.

The results obtained from the analysis (based mainly on a linear-programming technique) are subject to numerous caveats. In the first place, they represent partial-equilibrium solutions and disregard indirect effects and external economies or diseconomies. While the locations chosen are intended to reflect minimum-cost combinations, they cannot properly be called optimal. Furthermore, because exchange rates had to be taken as given, the cost comparisons are again in terms of absolute cost, and do not pretend to reflect comparative advantage (which would have involved providing for equilibration of the balance of payments through exchange-rate adjustments). This is a limitation of the study, given the volatility of Latin American exchange-rate relationships. However, in order to cope with this problem, the data were processed not only at the official exchange rates prevailing on the dates costs were measured, but also at "free" rates of exchange, where these existed. Moreover, in addition to deriving minimum-cost locations for both minimum and maximum sets of transport costs and exchange rates, another calculation was made in order to estimate "indifference" rates of exchange (showing that rate of exchange between two producer countries at which a consumer country is indifferent as to whether it imports a given product from either of the producers). In effect, these indifference exchange rates (analogous to a shadow-price of foreign exchange) show the sensitivity of the ranking of the optimal-location solutions to exchange-rate changes. This sensitivity is less in those locations where the country's comparative advantage is large.

Another important feature of the Brookings/ECIEL analysis is that it can take account of such considerations as favoring the relatively less-advanced countries, since it is possible to evaluate the order of magnitude of the welfare loss involved in locating an industry in a less-than-optimal country.

It is impossible to summarize, in the space available here, the detailed results of this exercise, as far as locations of the incremental plants for the individual industries are concerned, because alternative solutions were obtained depending on whether minimum or maximum assumptions were used for the parameters cranked into the model. Among the more significant general conclusions, it can be mentioned that the study found scale effects to be sufficiently important to make LAFTA production competitive with imports from third countries under integration conditions. Another encouraging result is that no one country has an absolute advantage all around; six or seven LAFTA countries appear as minimum-cost suppliers in producing one or more of the fourteen products studied. Moreover, it turned out that many of the nonoptimal solutions differed from the optimum by only a few per cent. This indicated that, in such cases, the political decisions to locate industries in the "wrong" countries would not necessarily involve serious economic costs to the region.

Summarizing the results of the aggregative welfare calculations, and assuming that the six industry groups studied are representative of the manufacturing sector in Latin America, the estimated gain from producing at minimum-cost locations within LAFTA in 1975 as compared with buying from the U.S. implies a net annual gain of 4 per cent of GDP in real resources for Latin America, equivalent to an increase of 0.6 per cent in the growth rate of the region. While the authors admit that this estimate is probably too high, it indicates that a common market within LAFTA "may have important implications for making Latin American producers competitive in world market."[22]

Another quantitative "welfare" finding of the study measures the estimated cost of autarky at the national level as compared with buying from the minimum-cost locations within LAFTA. This turns out to be the equivalent of about $200 million per annum for the six industry groups studied. Finally, it is also estimated that the welfare cost in 1975 of maintaining the existing national tariff structures would amount to about half a billion dollar-equivalent for the six industry groups.

Among other methodological problems affecting these results, it may be noted that no attempt was made to deflate the base prices of domestically produced inputs to take account of price distortions resulting from the existing tariff structure. This implies that lowering tariffs between Latin American countries does not change the production cost curves at each location. It is recalled that similar problems arise when effective protection estimates are based on data from domestic input-output tables, which themselves reflect the distortions resulting from the national protective structure.

The complexities of the Brookings/ECIEL model were already such that no attempt was made to go beyond the domain of partial equilibrium analysis. A more elaborate model, with more endogenous variables, may be much more satisfying intellectually, but at any significant level of disaggregation by products and countries, it quickly gets out of hand computationally. It may be of interest to note, in passing, a macroeconomic model designed by Rolf Mantel, an Argentine economist, that was intended to give a relatively complete theoretical analysis of integration effects.[23] It distinguished only three productive sectors (agriculture, industry, and services) for four geographic areas

(Argentina, Brazil, Chile, and "rest of the world"). The computer program had to solve 11 systems of 240 equations each. Most of the equations were in differential form, indicating the direction of change of the dependent variables, but not the absolute change. The author rightly cautioned against putting any credence in the actual results, given the level of aggregation of the model, but the experiment illustrated the types of interdependent relationships that would have to be taken into account in evaluating the total effects of a process of economic integration. These variables included the relative price levels, the balance of trade, rates of consumption, employment, and national income. In order to derive realistic results, one would have to take account of a number of disaggregated industrial sectors. Among the many additional statistical series required, it would be necessary to have disaggregated estimates of the price disparities corresponding to the protective barriers being dismantled, as well as interindustry input-output data.

IMPLICATIONS OF INTEGRATION FOR INTERNATIONAL FIRMS

It is well know that the increased industrial interpenetration of national European markets that occurred during the formation of the Common Market was accomplished to a large extent by multinational firms (predominantly U.S. direct-investment companies). For a number of legal, institutional, financial, technological, and management reasons, they were in a far better position to implement production and marketing strategies in a regional framework than were the European-owned national firms. A strong school of European thought holds that the principal beneficiaries of European integration have been American companies.

Similarly, such industrial integration as has occurred to date in Latin America has largely involved either wholly owned subsidiaries of international companies or multinational joint ventures in which U.S. or other foreign extrazonal firms played the dominant role. Quite aside from the historical position of foreign investment in Latin America and longstanding political and psychological attitudes, it is understandable that Latin Americans, even more than Europeans, should be under the impression that regional integration schemes are primarily for the benefit of foreign corporations. In Europe, the phenomenon of intraindustry specialization has accompanied the automatic reduction of trade barriers in the region, and international firms could claim that they were merely taking advantage of an opening-up of market opportunities that were available to all comers.

In Latin American integration schemes, however, there is an

additional element making for greater visibility of the foreign firms'
role: the element of special privilege under the aegis of governmental
and intergovernmental authority. Participation in the CACM integration-
industry scheme involves an explicitly sanctioned monopoly position,
and participation in a LAFTA complementarity agreement involves
hand-tailored arrangements that also have de facto monopolistic
features. These are in addition to the generous privileges--tax holidays, rapid write-off, customs derogations on inputs, etc.--given as
investment incentives by the individual governments.

This situation faces both the foreign companies and the host
governments with uncomfortable dilemmas. The companies are
damned if they do and damned if they don't play a conspicuous role in
integration-related investment activity. The governments would
prefer to give the privileges to indigenous firms, but they usually
have no choice but to look to the foreign firms for the combination of
capital and know-how needed to establish the new plants. The special
privileges are, however, likely to be hedged about with particularly
restrictive conditions. It is recalled that the rules governing Central
American integration industries not only lay down special conditions
as to capacity, guaranty of market supply, and selling prices, but also--
and most significantly--with respect to composition of corporate ownership. The GINSA tire enterprise had a 50-50 ownership composition,
while the caustic soda and chlorinated insecticides industry only had
to have 40 per cent Central American capital. However, the proportion
provided for in the 1965 protocol on the window and plate glass industry
was 60 percent. A similar trend is observed in LAFTA. The first
complementarity agreement (1962) involved 100 per cent-owned subsidiaries of IBM. On the other hand, the petrochemicals agreement
(No. 6, 1968) envisaged harmonization of the treatment of foreign
capital and establishment of a regime for creation and regulation of
multinational firms, which in this context meant joint ventures.

The most sensitive aspect of the problem of the status of
foreign enterprises in Latin America relates to the extent of local
participation and to the locus of decision-making. There is no doubt
that the pressures for formation of joint ventures are increasing, and
that these will be particularly cogent in the context of coordination of
investment policies in the framework of the regional and subregional
integration schemes.

These tensions are also coming to a head in a broader context
than that of the special legal provisions under the integration regimes.
The views of Aldo Ferrer appear to be indicative of moderate Latin
American opinion.*

---

*Ferrer was subsequently appointed Argentine minister of

It is interesting to observe that this problem of the
"alienation" of the centers of decision becomes really
important from the moment when the process of import
substitution begins to weaken and there is an inescapa-
ble necessity to export manufactured goods so as to
overcome external strangulation and facilitate the
continued integration of the industrial structures. To
the extent that the national economy participates more
actively in international trade in manufactures, the
power of decision of the head offices with respect to
the location and extension of plants, export of manufactures, technological progress, and other matters
acquires greater importance. . . . It is vital to know,
then, who will be making those decisions and in response
to what motivations. Will it be the responsible authorities of the country seeking to promote the aspirations
of the national community or will there be centers of
decision located outside the frontiers which will decide
in accordance with their own global development
strategy?

In the import-substitution phase the problem was
less acute. The decisions of the international corporations were obviously influenced by such domestic determinants as size of market, level of tariff protection,
national promotional policies, and the dynamics of
national development in a market that was increasingly
cut off from external competition and that did not par-
ticipate in international trade in manufactured goods.

. . . Within an autarkic import-substitution model
it is probably possible to have coexistence of a high
participation of foreign capital in the principal industrial sectors along with preservation of the national
character of decisions on the development of such
sectors.[24]

Ferrer went on to argue that Argentina could not afford to exclude the
foreign firms, but that it would be justified in taking concrete measures
to strengthen the position of national firms in the more dynamic industries, e.g., by giving them fiscal and credit incentives, and especially
by promoting formation of joint ventures. In addition, he suggested

---

public works (August, 1970) and minister of economic affairs (October,
1970) in the Levingston Government.

using public procurement for the same purpose and reserving certain fields of investment to national firms. At the same time, measures should be taken to stimulate the foreign firms to export and to renounce restrictive practices that might limit subsidiaries' freedom of action in this respect. In Ferrer's view, the international corporations will accept such conditions in order to avoid exclusion from a market of the size of Argentina.

There are others, however, who are more dubious about whether those international firms that have the most to offer in technology and international marketing ability will accept the joint-venture formula under such terms.[25]* Raymond Vernon has analyzed the dynamics of the shifts in bargaining power between the international company and the host country. Unified control, he says, is most important to those international companies engaged in extractive raw-material industries. On the other hand, in the case of import-substituting manufacturing industries, foreign firms will more readily accept a preponderance of local participation. (But, as Ferrer pointed out, this is precisely the situation where the host countries have least objection to 100 per cent-foreign-ownership situations). Once the host country begins to seek export markets for its manufactures (other than standardized products like textile piece-goods), the advantages of strong head-office control and a centralized marketing strategy again come to predominate. This changing bargaining situation tends to exacerbate the current tensions. Vernon suggests that these could be alleviated if it were agreed between the parties that initial arrangements would remain undisturbed for a fixed period of time, provided the termination date, "while distant, was not remote," a period that might range from seven to 20 years. He admits that such a rule would be hard to apply in a specific practical case, so he closes his argument on the inspirational note that "Here is a neglected opportunity for institution-building in the interests of economic development."[27]

In the Latin American regional organizations, the problems of such institution-building are the object of intensive study. The Organization of American States[28] has shown interest in the Vernon proposal

---

*R. M. Moore finds that international firms " would like to integrate Latin America, but want to do it on the basis of decisions made solely in their home countries. The conclusion is that unless they are willing to regionalize their enterprises allowing public or private 'local' investors to have meaningful participation in decisions and profits, they will not be integrative forces but rather will continue to give the governments one of their strongest reasons to reject integration."[26]

and a similar proposal by Paul N. Rosenstein-Rodan whereby, as a
general rule, fully or majority-owned foreign equity in joint ventures
would be limited in time, although "it is important to induce foreign
investors to maintain a substantial (say 40 per cent) and not only a
small minority holding, especially in those sectors in which the flow
of new technology depends on their headquarters."[29] The same general
notion, that provision should be made for planned, eventual repatriation
of foreign ownership in direct investments in Latin America, has also
been advanced by Albert O. Hirschman.[30]*

    A solution that finds still more favor among the Latin American
técnicos is that of the Latin American multinational firm, which,
according to one of its principal proponents, "would operate regionally
or subregionally and in which the Latin American public sector would
have a decisive participation either directly (capital contribution and
control of decisions) or indirectly (creation of stimuli and mechanisms
to strengthen the private sector)."[31] Such enterprises (also referred
to as "zonal-multinational" as distinguished from "multinational-extra-
zonal" and "multinational-zonal" firms) could include some minority
extrazonal participation, so long as the latter did not have control.
Existing examples of such enterprises that are frequently referred to
are the Flota Gran Colombiana (Colombia-Ecuador) and the Central
American Corporation for Aerial Navigation Services (COCESNA).
Outside the region, the British Commonwealth Pacific Airlines Ltd.,
Air Afrique, and SAS airlines are also taken as models worthy of
imitation.[32] Whether or not this is a realistic formula, the attention
now being devoted to it reflects the strong concern of many Latin
Americans lest integration turn out to be sucursalización.[33]

    It has been observed above that Latin American and other
developing countries are likely to be most receptive to foreign direct-
investment capital on the companies' own terms, during the phase of
national-level import-substitution policy. On the other hand, when the
countries begin to look outward, as at present, and begin to think about
exporting nontraditional manufactured products within an integration
area or toward third countries, they tend to impose more stringent
conditions on the foreign companies. In general, import-substitution
policy appears to have been used as a justification for relatively

---

    *In December, 1970, the five members of the Andean Common
Market reportedly decided to limit foreign ownership of regional companies to 49 per cent. In Peru, Chile, and Colombia, foreign companies
will have 15 years in which to turn over 51 per cent to nationals. In
the less-developed countries, Bolivia and Ecuador, the time limit will
be 29 years. (Wall Street Journal, December 28, 1970.)

favorable treatment of foreign capital. One may well ask whether the converse is true, i.e., is the desire to encourage a capital inflow a valid reason for setting high levels of effective protection in those sectors in which it is desired to attract foreign capital? The answer of economic theory appears to be clearly negative. W. M. Corden has shown that a nonoptimum tariff system may cause a social loss from capital inflow. It is best to improve the tariff system, even at the cost of foregoing foreign investment. Given a nonoptimal (i.e., protective) tariff system, Corden advocates taxing or controlling capital inflow.[34] A similar conclusion was reached, on more empirical grounds, in the study of the OECD Development Center on industrialization, which found no support for the proposition that heavy protection is required to attract foreign capital and which also noted that a country can attract too much foreign capital.[35]

Views expressed by Raúl Prebisch in his recent report to Felipe Herrera may be of interest in these regards. According to Prebisch, each country should designate the fields in which it is seeking direct investments and lay down the regime that would govern them. Emphasizing balance-of-payments considerations, he says that foreign investment must contribute to exporting and to import substitution. Given the very limited possibilities for national-level import substitution, arrangements for integration must be made in which Latin American initiative should play the dominant role except in those cases where, because of the need for new technologies, it is considered appropriate to open the door wider to foreign private investment.[36]

PROBLEMS OF HARMONIZING PROTECTIVE
STRUCTURES

It has long been clear that the process of mutual trade liberalization within LAFTA, as originally envisaged in the Treaty of Montevideo, is grinding to a halt. It is more and more difficult to make concessions on a most-favored-nation-within-LAFTA basis through item-by-item negotiations under the National List procedure, while the Common List procedure appears to have stalled on the interrelated bargaining problems of agriculture and oil. At present, the main avenues for further movement in the LAFTA framework appear to be via the sectoral approach (complementarity agreements) and the sub-regional approach (Andean Group). These have two features in common: first, conditional rather than unconditional most-favored-nation treatment (i.e., countries other than those deemed relatively less advanced will not automatically receive concessions not paid for by reciprocal concessions), which leads to geographical compartmentalization within LAFTA, and second, provision for establishment of common external tariffs on both outputs and inputs.

        The objective of moving from a free-trade area to a common
market (i.e., a customs union, implying common external tariffs) was
laid down in the preamble of the Treaty of Montevideo, although only
the ECLA Secretariat took this goal very seriously at the time. (The
original interest in LAFTA on the part of the major participating countries was mainly that of finding a GATT-able way of restoring the intra-
area trade that had taken place through bilateral trade and payments
agreements until the mid-1950's.) The goal of a common market,
based on the principle of reciprocity, was reaffirmed by the report of
the "Four Wise Men" in 1965, in answer to the appeal of President
Eduardo Frei of Chile, and it was subsequently embodied in the Action
Program laid down by the Declaration of American Presidents at Punta
del Este, Uruguay, on April 14, 1965. Since then, however, not even
lip service has been given to the common-market ideal in LAFTA
deliberations by the major countries--Argentina, Brazil, and Mexico--
which have apparently never been particularly interested in regional
economic integration other than in the form of establishment of margins
of mutual tariff preferences insofar as these might be useful to their
respective interest groups. While opportunities for improving economies of scale would be welcome, these three countries already have
domestic markets of sufficient size that no urgent need for far-reaching
regional trade liberalization is felt. To the extent that the Andean
Group gives promise of diverting the common-market notion away
from the main stream of LAFTA activity, its creation did not disturb
the Big Three. Meanwhile, the LAFTA Secretariat has also been
extremely reticent about any plans for a common external tariff,
except to the extent that tariff harmonization toward third countries
is involved in complementarity agreements on a very piecemeal basis.
Reflecting the general lack of enthusiasm, the LAFTA Conference held
in Caracas in 1969 put off even the free-trade-area target from 1973
to 1980. The interim period from 1970 to 1980 is to be devoted mainly
to studies, designated as an Action Plan (!). Even within the study
program, studies and recommendations with respect to margins of
preference get priority. Customs treatment of third countries is
relegated to relatively minor importance, although mention is still
made--in passing--of the ultimate "possibility" of establishing a
common external tariff.[37]

        Regardless of these and other difficulties of moving toward a
common external tariff,[38] the author is convinced that significant
further trade liberalization within the free-trade-area framework
would be still more difficult, if not impossible. In addition to all the
frustrations of item-by-item negotiation, as provided for in the Treaty
of Montevideo, any free-trade area is plagued by the problem that
trade, production, and investment will be displaced unless the process
of trade liberalization is hedged about with so many "rules of origin"
that it becomes hardly worthwhile. Displacement of trade occurs

because products are likely to be imported from third countries through
low-tariff members and then transhipped to high-tariff members. Displacement of production occurs when final products, manufactured by
countries having low external tariffs on inputs, are sold in countries
having higher input costs. This, in turn, eventually leads to displacement
of investment.[39] The methods of avoiding such displacement of trade,
production, and investment involve establishment of origin criteria
based on a minimum percentage of value added, or on a specified type
of national processing, supplemented sometimes by designations of
those inputs arbitrarily considered to be of area origin whether they
are or not. Otherwise, compensatory taxes must be applied on intra-
area trade, which is inconsistent with the goal of integration.

     The origin problem has been manageable within EFTA, where
post-Kennedy Round national external tariffs on inputs and outputs are
relatively low by South American standards. Within LAFTA, where
tariffs on raw materials are 50 to 100 per cent or more in some countries and zero in others, a satisfactory resolution of the origin problem
seems hopeless except as applied to a few products in the framework,
say, of sectoral complementarity agreements. Even here, provision
for common external tariffs is becoming the preferred solution.

     If there is to be meaningful integration, therefore, and not just
a system of mutual preferences almost as ad hoc as those that would
probably otherwise be negotiated under bilateral trade agreements,
there must be progressive harmonization of external tariffs tending
in the direction of common external tariffs. There is still a great
deal to be done within LAFTA in reconciling nomenclatures, rules of
valuation, etc., before serious work on setting target ad valorem tariff
levels can proceed very far. Nevertheless, the crux of the technical
problem is the confrontation of tariff profiles both in terms of broad
aggregates and, ultimately, item-by-item. Thus far, the work of the
LAFTA study group on the Common External Tariff has consisted
mainly of collecting the sample information to which reference has
already been made. The deliberations of the group are naturally not
in the public domain, but the author has seen little evidence that the
interpretation of the data obtained from the muestra experimental
has progressed very far.

     As a result of the formation of the Andean Group, the sub-
regional approach to Latin American integration has come to the fore.
To be sure, this is officially envisioned as being still within the framework of the Treaty of Montevideo and, since the Declaration of the
American Presidents, of a slow but steady movement--to be completed
by 1985--toward a Latin American common market comprising both
LAFTA and the CACM and possibly also other countries of the region
not included in either group (Panama, Haiti, Dominican Republic, the

CARIFTA* grouping, ultimately Cuba?). The precise route toward
realization of this grand design has not as yet been mapped out. This
is fortunate, because there are many possible permutations and combinations of subregional groupings. Even the ultimate composition of the
Andean Group is uncertain. Political and cultural factors are obviously
important, if not the dominant considerations. However, there are also
more technical factors, not least of which are those resulting from the
nature of the existing disparities of protective structure among the
individual countries and among the possible groupings.

In making political judgments about the future of the integration
movement in Latin America, therefore, it is necessary to have a reasonably clear picture of what these major differences in protective structure actually are, since these will play an obvious role in evaluating
the feasibility and relative likelihood of alternative courses of events.
Confrontation of the respective protective profiles and their implications
for relative prices, on the basis of the best available data, will give a
preliminary indication of the obstacles to harmonization and of the
nature of the possible alignment processes. Among the important
questions that should be examined is that of whether alignment is more
likely to occur, if at all, on the basis of some sort of averaging of
existing protective structures (as in the EEC) or whether an entirely
new common tariff structure would have to be constructed from the
ground up. Whether or not averaging of national tariffs is a practical
basis for negotiation of common tariffs, calculation of such averages
by several different methods (e.g., simple average, simple average
with extreme tariffs omitted, averages omitting certain countries,
averages in which certain countries are weighted more heavily) can
be a valuable analytical tool for evaluating the dimensions of the problem.

It has not been possible to embark on such a comprehensive
comparative analysis in the framework of this study. Much more
study, more data, and more manipulation of the available data would
be required. The following are merely very tentative conclusions,
derived mainly from inspection of partial profiles of nominal protection
for 11 LAFTA countries, as compared with the simple arithmetic
averages for the group as a whole (with and without inclusion of the
highest and lowest tariffs for each category):[40]

1. Wide disparities among the protective structures of the
LAFTA region make formation of a common market--i.e. harmonization
of protection-induced ratios between domestic and world prices--a much

---

*The Caribbean Free Trade Association (CARIFTA), established
on May 1, 1968, consists of 11 Commonwealth countries and territories
in the Caribbean archipelagos.

more formidable objective, requiring a higher degree of political
motivation, than was the case with the Central American Common
Market, let alone the European Economic Community.

2. The problems of chronic inflation and currency overvaluation are serious additional complications in most of the countries of
the LAFTA area. However, to the extent that countries resort to
frequent devaluations during the transitional stage, the alignment of
levels of protection will be facilitated. (See Chart 16, showing the
evolution of Brazil's structure of exchange rates and protection.)

3. Countries having particularly high and/or erratic tariff
structures as compared with the LAFTA average (or the Andean Group
average) should unilaterally reform their entire protective and exchange
systems at the national level (preferably using compensated devaluations) before committing themselves too far on any particular process
of regional (or subregional) harmonization of tariffs toward third
countries. Similarly, countries now relying on multiple exchange
rates, customs surcharges, and quantitative restrictions should first
absorb these into their tariff systems (preferably expressed in ad
valorem terms).

4. Since it would be relatively less differentiated, a common
external tariff based on an averaging of national tariffs would probably
be better, from the resource-allocational standpoint, than one constructed according to "scientific" import-substitution principles or
negotiated item by item.

5. Any attempt to bind margins of intra-LAFTA preference
based on present national protective structures should be avoided,
since it would hamstring rational formulation of a common external
tariff. Premature establishment of external tariffs on a piecemeal
sectoral basis (as is occurring under complementarity agreements)
also has the disadvantage of prejudging the ultimate common external
tariff.

6. The failure to date to make really substantial progress in
intra-LAFTA trade liberalization has at least had the advantage of
avoiding the creation of entrenched vested interests in deep margins
of intrazonal preferences, such as would appear if zero nominal protection were applied on important trade categories for which the
present most-favored-nation rates are extremely high. For this
reason, as well as for pragmatic political reasons, the author sees
much merit in the approach now being advocated by the UNCTAD
Secretariat:[41] viz., setting of moderate "intermediate targets" of
intra-area trade liberalization and, particularly, substitution of
ceilings to protection for the objective of complete dismantlement of
protective measures within the zone.

NOTES

1. Tariff averages by categories, based on an ECLA sample study, are conveniently tabulated in Andrew B. Wardlaw, Achievements and Problems of the Central American Common Market (U.S. Dept. of State, February, 1969), p. 46. See also ECLA, Estado General y Perspectivas del Programa de Integración Económica del Istmo Centro americano (E/CN. 12/CCE/265, January 12, 1963), pp. 21-27. The method used in formulating the common tariff is described in Porfirio Morera Batres, "El Arancel de Aduanas del Mercado Común Centroamericano" in "El Arnacel de Aduanas del Mercado Comun Centro-Latina, op. cit., pp. 295-322.

2. For texts of these agreements and their protocols, see Inter-American Institute of International Legal Studies, Instruments Relating to the Economic Integration of Latin America (Dobbs Ferry, N.Y.: Oceana Publications, 1968).

3. For a study of the GINSA experience, see David E. Ramsett, Regional Industrial Development in Central America: A Case Study of the Integration Industries Scheme (New York: Frederick A. Praeger, 1969), Appendix A.

4. The regulations for this scheme were included in Chapter 4 of the first protocol to the Agreement on the System of Central American Integrated Industries.

5. Roger D. Hansen, Central America: Regional Integration and Economic Development, Studies in Development Progress, No. 1 (Washington, D.C.: National Planning Association, 1967), p. 61. Hansen continues: "The U.S. Government's insistence upon applying dubious economic criteria alone in evaluating the Integration-Industries System reveals both an inability to comprehend the conflicted nature of the Central American historical experience and a resulting misapplication of a purely technocratic approach in its otherwise well-intentioned and generous support of the Common Market."

6. For brief descriptive reviews of this system, see Edward G. Cale, Latin American Free Trade Association: Progress, Problems, Prospects (A report prepared under contract for the Office of External Research, U.S. Dept. of State, May, 1969), pp. 20-24; Ann Tonjes, The Role of "Complementarity" Agreements in LAFTA (Overseas Business Reports, U.S. Dept. of Commerce, OBR 68-11, March, 1968); ALALC, "La integración industrial. Acuerdos de complementación," Síntesis Mensual, V, 47 (May, 1969).

7. Donald W. Baerresen, Martin Carnoy, and Joseph Grunwald, Latin American Trade Patterns (Washington, D.C.: The Brookings Institution, 1965), p. 38.

8. Instruments Relating to the Economic Integration of Latin America, op. cit., pp. 303-04.

9. ALALC, Secretaría, Bases para la complementación del Sector Siderúrgico en la ALALC (CEP/GE.S/III/dt 1, 13 March 1969); La Industria petroquímica en la ALALC (ALALC/CG.PQ/1/dt 1, 16 April 1969); La Industria de papel y celulosa en la ALALC (CEP/GE. /IV/dt 1, 18 June 1969); Estudio sobre fertilizantes en los países de la ALALC (CEP/GE.FER/I dt 1, 19 May 1969). The study entitled La Industria automotriz en la ALALC, also completed in May, 1969, is summarized in ALALC, Síntesis mensual, 58 (April, 1970), 128-54. A study of the agricultural machinery sector has also been initiated.

10. ALALC, Apreciaciones sobre el proceso de Integracion de la ALALC (Montevideo: Asociación Latino Americana de Libre Comerico, 1969), pp. 50-51.

11. The deplorable present situation of the Latin American automotive industry has been abundantly documented. Cf. Jack Baranson, Automotive Industries in Developing Countries, World Bank Occasional Papers No. 8, IBRD (Baltimore: Johns Hopkins Press, 1969), pp. 35-52; Bernard Munk, "The Welfare Cost of Content Protection: The Automotive Industry in Latin America," Journal of Political Economy, (January-February, 1969), 85-97; Leland L. Johnson, "Problems of Import Substitution: The Chilean Automobile Industry," reprinted from Economic Development and Cultural Change (January, 1967), pp. 202-16, reprinted in Charles T. Nisbet, Latin America: Problems in Economic Development (New York: Free Press, 1969).

12. Aldo Ferrer, "Hacia un sistema industrial integrado y abierto," El Cronista Comercial (Buenos Aires, special edition, December, 1968), pp. 3-7.

13. ECLA, The United Nations Second Development Decade: Industrial Development in Latin America (E/CN.12/830 of 1969), p. 163.

14. For a more comprehensive account of ECLA's proposals for industrial agreement in the framework of Latin American integration, see "Contribución a la politica de integración económica de America Latina: Studio técnico de CEPAL" in Hacia la integración acelerada de America Latina: Proposiciones a los Presidentes

Latinoamericanos presentadas por J. A. Mayobre, Felipe Herrera, Carlos Sanz de Santamaria, Raúl Prebisch (México: Fondo de Cultura Economica, 1965, pp. 121-81.

15. Informal memo from the LAFTA Adviser, U.S. Embassy, Montevideo.

16. The only public information available on the study is in J. M. Dagnino Pastore and J. C. de Pablo, Los costos industriales en las industrias básicas y el nivel de eficiencia de la industria en los países latinoamericanos (Buenos Aires: BID/INITAL, Seminar on "Desarrollo Nacional e Integración Regional en America Latina," November 25 to 29, 1968).

17. Ayhan Çilingiroğlu, Manufacture of Heavy Electrical Equipment in Developing Countries, World Bank Staff Occasional Paper No. 9 (Baltimore: Johns Hopkins Press, 1969).

18. Baranson, Automotive Industries in Developing Countries, op. cit., pp. 35-42

19. Ibid., p. 39.

20. Ana Maria Martirena Mantel, Integracion y Economías de Escala, Documento de Trabajo No. 19, 2nd ed., (Buenos Aires: Instituto Torcuato de Tella, 1966). (An earlier version was published in Trimestre Económico [July-September, 1964], pp. 412-22).

21. Martin Carnoy, ed., Industrialization in a Latin American Common Market (Washington, D.C.: The Brookings Institution, 1968); see note 18 to Chapter 7, above.

22. Carnoy, "A Welfare Analysis. . . .," op. cit., p. 245.

23. Rolf Mantel, Un modelo neo-clásico de integración económica, Documento de trabajo No. 20, 2a edicion (Buenos Aires: Instituto de Tella, 1966).

24. Ferrer, op. cit., p. 8. (Free translation.)

25. Miguel S. Wionczek, "A Latin American View," in Raymond Vernon, ed., How Latin America Views the U. S. Investor (New York: Frederick A. Praeger, 1966); Sidney E. Rolfe, The International Corportion (XXIInd Congress of the International Chamber of Commerce, Istanbul, May 31-June 7, 1969), pp. 66-72. For further discussion of the merits and demerits of joint ventures, see Dirk U. Stikker, The Role of Private Enterprise in Investment and Promotion of Exports in

Developing Countries (UNCTAD document TD/35 and TD/35, Supp. 1, November 16, 1967)Chapter 2; and J. S. Ramaer (of the Philips concern), International Joint Business Ventures in Developing Countries (UNCTAD document TD/B/NGO/9, January 9, 1969.

26. Russell M. Moore, The Role of Extrazonally Controlled Multinational Corporations in the Process of Establishing Regional Latin American Automotive Industry: A Case Study of Brazil (unpublished Ph.D. dissertation, Fletcher School of Law and Diplomacy, September, 1969), Preface.

27. Raymond Vernon, "Conflict and Resolution between Foreign Direct Investors and Less Developed Countries," Public Policy, XVII (1968), 340. See also other works of Vernon on "the multinational firm," notably: "International Trade and International Investment in the Product Cycle," Quarterly Journal of Economics, 80 (May, 1966).

28. General Secretariat of the Organization of American States, The Role of Foreign Private Investment in the Development of Latin America (OEA/Ser. H/X. 14, CIES/1371, 28 April 1969), p. 7.

29. Paul N. Rosenstein-Rodan, "Multinational Investment in the Framework of Latin American Integration" in Inter-American Development Bank, Multinational Investment, Public and Private, in the Economic Development and Integration of Latin America, Round Table (Bogotá, April, 1968), p. 77.

30. Albert O. Hirschman, How to Divest in Latin America, and Why, Essays in International Finance, No. 76 (Princeton, N.J.: International Finance Section, Princeton University, November, 1969).

31. Gustavo Lagos (director, INTAL), "Socio-economic, Legal and Institutional Aspects of Multinational Enterprises," in IADB, Multinational Investment ..., op. cit., p. 213.

32. Ibid., p. 227; "Emprêsa Multinacional," O Globo-Economico (Rio de Janeiro, November 29, 1969).

33. Osvaldo Sunkel, quoted by Rosenstein-Roda, op. cit., p. 35.

34. W. M. Corden, "Protection and Foreign Investment," Economic Record, 43, 102 (May, 1967), 209-32.

35. Ian Little, Tibor Scitovsky, and Maurice Scott, Industry and Trade in Some Developing Countries (London: Oxford University Press, 1970), pp. 202-5.

36. Raúl Prebisch, Transformación y Desarrollo: La gran tarea de América Latina (Santiago: Instituto Latinoamericano de Planificación Económica y Social, April 17, 1970), pp. 109-14.

37. See text of Resolution 206 in "Prioridades del Plan de Acción de la ALALC, 1970-1980," ALALC, Síntesis mensual, 61 (July, 1970), 310-26.

38. Some of the technical problems of approaching common external tariffs are illuminated in the following sources: Gustavo Magariños, "Los instrumentos de la integración y le experiencia de la ALALC," In Wionczek, Integración de America Latina, op. cit., pp. 115-35; Calderón, op. cit., pp. 115-35; Hugo Opazo, "La armonización de los sistemas aduaneros de los paises de la ALALC," in INTAL, Hacia un Tarifa Externa Común en America Latina, op. cit., pp. 105-48; ECLA, "Contribución a la Politica de Integración Económica de América Latina," in Hacia la Integración Acelerada de América Latina, op. cit., pp. 94-109.

39. Cf. Bela Balassa, The Theory of Economic Integration (Homewood, Ill.: Richard D. Irwin, 1961), cited by Calderón, op. cit., p. 41.

40. The data from which the profiles referred to were drawn were taken from various fascículos of the muestra experimental (experimental tariff-sample study) compiled by the LAFTA Secretariat from information supplied by the member countries. (See Chapter 3 for description.) This material is apparently still not in the public domain.

41. The UNCTAD Secretariat's suggestions were put forward in the Trade and Development Board's Intergovernmental Group on Trade Expansion, Economic Co-operation, and Regional Integration among Developed Countries, Geneva, November, 1970. See documents TD/B/AC.10/2 of September 9, 1970 and addenda 1 and 2 thereto dated October 7 and September 22, 1970, respectively.

163

Tan, A., 42 (n. 8), 43 (n. 15)
Tariff, common external
  in Central American Common
  Market, 131
  in European Economic Comuni-
  ty, 10-12
  in Latin American Free Trade
  Association, 152-55
Tariffs
  comparison of, 63-71
  escalation of, 30, 33, 102-3, 131
  implicit, 3
  measurement of, 44
  redundancy of, 3, 17, 152
Taxes
  border, 4-6
  export, 4, 92-93
  on value added (TVA), 5-6
Textiles, 139
Tinbergen, J., 88 (n. 17)
Tonjes, A., 156 (n. 6)
Trade
  creation and diversion, see Integration, economic gap, 84
  liberalization, intra-LAFTA, 112,
  134, 137, 151-52, 155
  terms of, 93, 100-101, 121, 124
Travis, W., 42 (n. 9), 59, 62 (n. 18,
  n. 20)
Turkey, 80

United Kingdom, 123
United Nations Conference on Trade
  and Development (UNCTAD), 10,
  32 (n. 13), 45, 49-51, 60 (n. 3), 84,
  94, 97-98, 109 (n. 19, 23), 110
  (n. 24), 116, 122, 126 (n. 8), 128
  (n. 20, 21), 130, 155, 160 (n. 41)
United Nations Department of Economic and Social Affairs, 83, 89
  (n. 28)
United Nations Organization for Industrial Development (UNIDO), 83

United Nations Statistical Office,
  86
Urdinola, A., and R. Mallon,
  71 (n. 2)
Urquidi, V., 83, 127 (n. 16)
Uruguay, 7, 20, 56-57, 71, 98,
  99, 136, 140, 141

Value added
  negative, 36
  ratios, 36-37
  tax on, 5-6
Vanek, J., 126 (n. 2, 5), 127
  (n. 13)
Venezuela, 7, 56-57, 70, 93, 100,
  140, 141
  Caracas, LAFTA Conference
  at (1969), 134, 152
Vernon, R., 149, 159 (n. 27)
Viner, J., 31 (n. 2), 113, 119,
  126 (n. 4)

Wardlaw, A., 156 (n. 1)
Weighting (of tariff averages),
  46-49
Williams College, 81, 88 (n. 23)
Winston, G., 88 (n. 23), 108 (n. 3,
  5)
Wionczek, M., 83, 158 (n. 25),
  160 (n. 38)

Yaounde Group, 116
Yeager, L., and D. Tuerck,
  86 (n. 1)
Yudelman, M., and F. Howard,
  110 (n. 27), 116-18, 127 (n. 9,
  11)

168

HARRY H. BELL is currently involved in independent consulting activity, based in Washington, D.C. His research interests are divided between international finance and commercial policy questions (notably, economic integration) and between problems of industrial countries and those of the developing areas of the world.

Following a career in the Foreign Service, during which he specialized in economic and financial assignments at various U.S. diplomatic posts, as well as in the U.S. State and Treasury Departments, he was given a three-year tour as Director of the Research Division of the United Nations Conference on Trade and Development (UNCTAD) in Geneva. He has participated in various international meetings, including UNCTAD's New Delhi Conference in 1968.

Mr. Bell did his undergraduate work at Haverford College, followed by a year at the Institut Universitaire de Haute Etudes Internationales in Geneva. Further academic studies, at Berkeley, the Air War College, and at universities in the Washington area, were interspersed with his Foreign Service assignments.

Date Due